CARIBBEAN FOLK LEGENDS

CARIBBEAN FOLK LEGENDS
by
Theresa Lewis

Africa World Press, Inc.

P.O. Box 1892
Trenton, New Jersey 08607

Africa World Press, Inc.
P.O. Box 1892
Trenton, NJ 08607

Library of Congress Catalog Card Number: 89-81981

ISBN 0-86543-158-2 Cloth
      0-86543-159-0 Paper

Cover Design   Duo Productions
Cover Art   *Maracas Bay* by Boscoe Holder

Printed and Bound in Canada.

CONTENTS

FOREWORD

The Legendary Figures mentioned here are peculiar to Trinidad and Tobago where the French and Spanish have left their mark on its mythology — as can be seen from many of the names of these figures. Similar figures can be found in many of the other West Indian Islands but with different names; but in some of the French Islands such as Martinique or Guadeloupe. Some of the names would be almost identical with the French patois used for many of the figures in the myths of Trinidad. No doubt some of them may have been introduced there by the French landowners who once populated the island, long before the influx of natives from the neighbouring French colonies.

It is also possible that these names came into existence because the real storytellers were the Afro-French people who settled in Trinidad. The most popular myths were therefore built around the La Gahoos, La Jablesse and the Soucouya (see Glossary).

I have long been familiar with some of the legends involving these figures. Nevertheless, the tales in this book — with the exception of 'Damal' (not his correct name) — have all been entirely constructed by me using the familiar titles and following the pattern of what has been established as the particular role of the discarnate in question.

Stories were told to me by persons who claim to have either experienced what they narrated themselves, or what they had learned of an incident from those who had. Using these incidents the stories here were created: extended and duly embroidered, of course.

"The Seers", for instance, was born of a conversation in which it was stated by someone that he had "personally experienced the exorcism of a woman who had been speaking Spanish — although everyone present knew that she had never spoken this language in her life". The characters are my own creation, none being a composite of any one particular person whom I had met, or had known, but an amalgam of different characteristics of different people.

Despite the sophistication of our times we are still, basically, a storytelling people, and it is not unusual for a short comment to evoke a tall tale which some grandmother has had closetted in her mind for half-a-century.

The "Jumbie", for instance is a popular term used for any supposedly supernatural appearance. It is reputed to have been seen by many people and is claimed to be either the spirit of some dead person whom "the Seer" had once known, or perhaps just some wandering discarnate. Sightings of Jumbies, therefore, are no novelty to the islanders and any story about a specific incident could either remain in the same context over the years — depending on whether it is a sufficiently thrilling tale — or take on proportions its originator had never dreamed about.

English and European Fairy Tales are told side by side with these more exotic ones. Little Red Riding Hood and Cinderella are as familiar to the islander as the titles of local origin, thus creating a *melange* or, colloqually, a *Callaloo*, of rich mythical literature.

Again, research has shown that there are similarities in supernatural tales originating in Quebec, for instance, and some from Trinidad; thus reinforcing the universal link in mythology and in particular, some of the Trinidadian stories where the names of characters are mainly of French origin.

On the other hand, in sects of more ancient origin such as Shango (a relic of African religion brought to the island during slavery), the African Gods predominate and Afro-English words have remained the basics. But these are sects which deal with religion, rather than legends.

It is only during the past two decades that attempts have been made to document the legends of the West Indies. Word-of-mouth is still the more popular form of narration. There is, therefore, no specific legend per se, which constitutes a complete tale. But there are snippets of short incidents; that vary at times according to narrator and there are certain basic stories which are well known. Few full length stories will be found but again, many short stories incorporating the traits and antics of the best known legendary figures have now come into existence. Soon this shortcoming may be remedied, as some tales become better established through documentation. Solid *Legends* will exist rather than just the use of Legendary Figures to create separate tales. This can become the icing on the cake and the filling in-between as it provides a greater scope for more interesting reading and the stories can be as varied as possible but more importantly, real Legends might come into existence as part of the basic literary culture of the islands.

Theresa Lewis

THE SEERS

Mama Rose's huge, well-rounded bosom looked as if it could encompass all the love in Africa which was reflected in her smooth, black face. The graceful haughtiness of her carriage might well have been a rightful bequest from royal ancestry. Perfect white teeth gleamed in a charming smile and her dark shining eyes were like windows which were kept spotlessly clean and which the visions of the outer world could not pierce. From behind them she herself looked out knowledgeably.

When Mama Rose became angry her eyes flashed and the beholder knew fear. She was proud of her African ancestry — a descendant of the Ashantis she proudly stated. This, no doubt, accounted for her regal bearing. Her son, Philip, whom everyone called Boyo, was a mixture of her own Ashanti and Zulu. A strange mixture, considering the geography of their original ancestors' homes, but slavery had brought about this conglomeration and Mama Rose was fortunate in knowing her origin and that of her son's, unlike many others who could not even attempt a guess at theirs.

Mama Rose had gone to Trinidad from Barbados when Philip was six, after she left his father: a fickle, shiftless young man.

Disheartened at her situation but strong in the resolution to find a better existence for them both, she had come there to work in the household of a rich family where eventually, she met and married their gardener, Ramon, a light-skinned mulatto of Spanish descent.

Older, and wiser, than Rose, he had given Philip what no natural father could have given more of: love, guidance, and a stable and secure home. There were no other children. When Ramon departed this life he continued, by whatever means the powers that be allow such matters, to guide and assist Mama Rose, now in her fifties, to continue in the role she had known her grandmother to follow during her early days in their tiny island. She was a clairvoyant and her son, no doubt by inheritance too, was also gifted in the art of witnessing intransient beings who remained invisible to those whose gift of sight was limited to the physical eye. Mama Rose and Boyo were "Seers". Gifted with the knowledge given to such people Mama Rose retained the means of curing those ill with varied maladies — both real and imaginary and more so, with the maladies attendant upon such as, either by accident or design, were ill-favoured enough to become haunted with the minds, and perhaps the ethereal bodies, of discarnates. Mama Rose was familiar with the use of herbs and with prayers for dispelling maladies of the body and mind, brought about by these discarnate beings who, for some selfish purpose, desired to continue inhabiting the earth long after their own bodies had become useless. With the laying on of her large, powerful hands, Mama Rose could heal both the willing and the unwilling.

After the death of Ramon she lived a religious life, and had a small following of people who gathered in her living room two or three nights a week to seek attunement with whatever existed in a more elevated form than their own miserable states, through prayers and hymn-singing.

To Mama Rose came mothers with anaemic babies who vomitted everything they tried to digest. To Mama Rose came young women who believed that they were being called to the veil of the convent but who, infected with doubts as to their own true motives and unwilling yet to depart from a life which held so many pleasures, sought her advice. Entranced by the spirit of the departed Ramon, Mama Rose advised the young mothers on what type of milk their babies could digest and how to cure the eczemas with which some were becoming infested through malnutrition with symptoms of Merasmee.

Mama Rose advised the young women to forget the young men who had caused them mental unrest and sufficient heartache to encourage thoughts of convents, or

9

suicide. When someone came who was possessed by a particularly virile entity, she enlisted Boyo's aid and went into trance while Boyo, with the necessary chants applicable to the particular case, and on the advice of his stepfather — through Mama Rose — entreated and cajoled, demanded or coerced the inopportune spirit to depart.

Such was the case with Melina, an incident long remembered by those who had heard, or personally witnessed the proceedings and who had related how Melina became possessed and how difficult it had been for Mama Rose and Boyo to free her.

Melina had been acting strangely. She lived in a small, neatly-kept two-bedroom house, which she had inherited from her parents. She was about 35 at the time and dearly loved children. She had never married. She adopted, so to speak, all and sundry who came within her reach. Melina had many and varied god-children and often took care of the babies nearby whose mothers wanted to go on errands. Loved by them all, in return her home was always lively with the rompings, laughter and happy cries of the young. She worked in a downtown restaurant and was reputed to be a good cook. Though her tiny followers needed no bribes to attract them, the tidbits she offered were an additional bonus.

When Melina first chased some of the children out of her house, vindictively demanding that they should stay away, this caused quite a stir. She had never been known to act in this way. A few hours later the same children were sought out and asked by Melina why they had not visited her. Consternation grew, as did her sudden and uncontrollable outbursts. One moment she would be laughing and cajoling — within another, like a schizoid on a double take she was shooing the children away, using language expected only of street rabble. Their parents became concerned, some forbidding their children to go over to Melina's, saying she was becoming prematurely senile. Others, more rational in their outlook, suggested she should see a doctor or take a rest, that perhaps she was overworked.

When reminded of her unpredictable actions Melina was amazed, having no recollection whatsoever of what she had done. These spells were brief at first — lasting only long enough to chase the children away, then, as time passed, the periods of her lapses lengthened, until one day Melina was heard ranting and raving as if she were involved in a fierce quarrel. Neighbours ran to her house. Melina was acting like a mad woman. Her hair wild, her eyes wilder, she gesticulated, laughed, cursed, spat at them, told them to leave her alone, and all the time it seemed as if it were not Melina but someone else who spoke. Her voice was heavier, her mannerisms different. Never one to use coarse language, it was all the more pathetic now to listen to her. Face distorted, sometimes she jumped up and down, sometimes she remained seated, when her body would stiffen while her arms continued waving and her eyes bulged. Sometimes she moved with lightning swiftness across the room to dash crockery against its walls; and threatening all the while to set the house afire if she were not left alone.

She stopped going to work. Whoever attempted to enter the house or to talk with her was rejected, though at times she seemed sufficiently reasonable. At those times she appeared exhausted and bewildered, looking around desperately as though she had lost something and would not ask about it, but wanted to find it herself, and pitifully, inquiring if something was wrong.

On occasions she lapsed into a strange dialect. At first people thought she was babbling incoherently, until they recognized that she was speaking Spanish. This was understood by one Martin Lezama who was present. He said that the words mean "You ... then a foul expression ... go parade in your own home, there is no carnival here."

Those present remained spellbound. They knew that it was not Melina speaking but some demon who had invaded her body. Melina would never, in two lifetimes, say such words to them. This new Melina was a parody of her true self. Furthermore, never to their knowledge did she ever speak Spanish or whatever strange gibberish escaped her now.

When Melina shouted out that her name was 'Lasso' and that she wanted her estate back, there was no doubt in anyone's mind but that her body had been invaded by the spirit of some long departed Spaniard. With Lezama in the audience, the despicable thing took the opportunity to spew out its vileness in Spanish. No one else understood and Lezama translated, to their great horror. Some wept. Some contradicted, saying that Lezama was having fun at their expense and that his interpretations were false. But having heard the equivalent in English they could not continue to deny that he was telling the truth.

Then came the time when Melina attempted to beat her head against the bedpost and there was no alternative to tying her down in order to prevent this.

She was a tall, slim, sun-bronzed woman with light brown eyes which complemented her mass of dark brown hair that had now lost any semblance of neatness and which stood out in every direction, its wiry curls untouched by a comb for many days. In school they had called her 'cat eyes' when her brown skin had not yet acquired the sun-darkened spots which now highlighted her prominent cheekbones.

It now took four people much effort to control her because she seemed to have gained the strength, ruthlessness and determination of three.

Lying still on the narrow bed where she had been secured she sometimes adopted a strange quietness, pleading to be untied and promising better behaviour. Wilyness was reflected in her eyes and on her drawn face. Her pleas were ignored, while the wisdom of fetching the local priest was being debated.

And this was how Boyo and Mama Rose found her when they arrived, her eyes moving shiftily from face to face then tracing a path from the thin curtains at the window to the far corner of the room where a large shelf on the wall, draped with cretonne, served as a wardrobe. Sometimes she pretended to be listening to the old woman who hugged one corner of the room, old Marie Denise, whose rosary of huge wooden beads trailed the length of her tey-ley-ley skirt while its crucifix dangled a dancing movement below. Spasmodic jerking of Melina's chin in the direction of the old woman indicated that she was aware of her presence and of her activity.

Suddenly a hush descended on the room, as if by a given signal. Wordlessly, Mama Rose walked to the bed and towered over it and its occupant. She fixed her gaze on Melina. Boyo, who had followed her in, stood watching closely, appearing to await some cue. He was as tall and as commanding in stature as his mother but with added strength to his every movement. His inscrutable round face would have seemed severe if it were not for the semblance of a smile which hovered at one corner of his thick lips. A quiet man who passed the time of day with many but claimed few as friends, he seemed somehow, like a huge shadow of Mama Rose. His wife Clementine, a tiny half-Indian, half-Negro woman, looked almost as a child beside him when they were out together and he had one of his large, capable, workman's hands around her shoulders.

Soon an unfathomable expression seemed to envelop Mama Rose's face and to create an indefinable featurelessness. Ramon was taking control. Her eyes became glazed, taking on a trance-like fixity. Melina's upraised eyes were cunningly glued to Mama Rose's face, fear tight in her unblinking gaze. But only for a second. Then their eyes seemed to lock as if each was demanding something of the other.

Without warning Mama Rose's right hand moved swiftly to deliver a stinging blow against Melina's cheek, the sound cutting through the tension in the room and reverberating like an echo in the minds of the audience. Everyone was startled. More so Melina who, after the initial surprise laughed hysterically, tauntingly, the thing in her calling out at one moment to be left alone, at another, after the second slap, that there was nothing anyone could do on earth or in heaven, that would make him leave the body — at least not until its death — that this was where he had chosen to stay, where he had found a space which could accommodate him after his long search.

Mama Rose said she would numb the body if this was the only way to be rid of him. There was a horrified gasp from those present, believing she meant "death". They wondered if she would carry things too far.

Then Mama Rose began to speak in a strange tongue and the listeners knew that, like Melina, it was really Ramon who was speaking through Mama Rose, commanding the unwanted entity to leave, as explained by Boyo, who moved up to stand in line with his mother. When she carried on in this strange dialect it was in direct reply to what Melina was saying. Her eyes on Mama Rose were unwavering. Sometimes she smiled cunningly as though she knew some secret the others did not. In fact, it was Lasso who spoke and smiled, not Melina. The strange dialect became punctuated at times with the Castilian patois Ramon had grown up speaking with his grandparents.

It appeared the unwanted guest was playing a game with the Ramon-controlled woman, trying to confuse her with his sudden change of language. And those in the room heard the strange unwelcome visitor speaking through Melina laugh scornfully at them, crying out "Ha ha ... you can't do a thing. You can't fool me ... you are all powerless, even with the spirit friend to help you, ha ha ... and the one with the beads ... ha ha. I know all about your fetishes and your beliefs. I took part in them once too."

Marie Denise was still hugging the corner and busily plying her beads.

Boyo left Mama Rose's side and went into the kitchen

while the others knelt and prayed quietly, each pair of lips moving hurriedly in its own private implorations.

Boyo returned with a cocoyea broom — the long, thin, brown flexes which had been stripped from the centre of the coconut palm leaves and held together with fine wire to create a broom. He started switching it lightly across Melina's body and brushing her face gently with it. But she just stared, never betraying that the hundred tips had any effect. As Mama Rose's incantation, which began softly, rose in volume, so did Boyo's lashings increase, becoming stronger, until he was whipping Melina in a frenzy but avoiding her face — just gently brushing against it with the broom — but lashing at her until she cried out, when he stopped, for it meant that he had reached the real Melina.

And Mama Rose stopped too. Her face was covered in perspiration that dripped down her forehead into her eyes and along her neck, glistening on her skin like tiny transparent pearls. And those who stayed to help, who had not been afraid to remain in an effort to give whatever assistance might be needed, felt the tears run down their faces for Melina, who did not deserve such a fate. They shared in the pain she should feel but apparently did not. Finally she lay there looking exhausted but still with that cunning smile hovering like an infant ghoul over a face which had only the accustomed lines of her familiar features.

Mama Rose would have to continue to seek help. She would have to consort more closely with Ramon. It was now three days since she and Boyo had been trying to oust Lasso and it was proving to be a difficult case indeed. While they thought they were managing from time to time to expel him, at least for short intervals, it was proved, eventually, that he had been quietly biding his time, pretending not to be there so that they would leave Melina alone. He was cleverly trying to fool them. During those times Melina achieved spasms of normalcy. Then suddenly there would come that sly smile and the calculating expression in her eyes when one could discern the personality of Lasso. Both Mama Rose and Boyo saw beyond Melina's face. They saw the overshadowing of heavy features.

Mama Rose would have to go into trance privately to seek advice from Ramon. Boyo would be at hand as the recorder.

Melina was slumped in the backseat of the old reconditioned Chev, one of the village's 'taxis'. She sat between Boyo who had one arm around her shoulders and Lezama, who held both her hands in his toughened, work-veined ones while Marie Denise, with a large rosary, sat squeezed beside Lezama. Melina's eyes moved calculatingly from one to the other. At least she was quiet. She had been quietening but no one really knew how much ground had been gained. They were continuing with plans as advised by Ramon, and Melina was on her way to the beach at Las Cuevas. Mama Rose sat at the front with the driver, Jojo, who was a younger second cousin of Ramon's. They would reach Las Cuevas just before it got dark. Melina would be dunked several times in the sea, after whatever simidimi it was necessary to perform.

Each day for the past three days Mama Rose and Boyo had gone to the house and burned incense, said prayers, commanded the unclean spirit to depart from Melina and had watched over her zealously. She had never been left alone for a moment. She had been spoonfed when quiet watered, washed and bedded down as convenient. Within those days they had got the full story of Lasso's life — and death. Born of German and French-Payole parents, his father, a German emigre to the island had owned numberless acres of land and had developed a large plantation. He married a woman of French and Spanish (Payole) descent. Her Spanish blood held a tincture from the Tar Brush. Lasso was therefore, a sort of Mongrel. But no one thought of people in those terms. You were either Spanishy or French; Mulatto or Bacchra — a white-skinned negro of indeterminate strains. You were Cheenwa — a dash or more of Chinese, or a Coolie — of East Indian descent. You were either a "brown-skin" or light skinned, or "very dark". You were white or, if uncertainly so, you were Bachra — perhaps like Lasso had been. He had had the good life, having inherited his father's estate together with other properties from his mother. He had married young and had fathered two sons and a daughter and kept servants who waited on him and his family hand-and-foot.

One day Lasso was found murdered on the grounds of his home. His throat had been cut. Many said his older son had done it. They had been known to fight occasionally. This son had developed a great dislike of him because of his well-known licentious behaviour. The murderer was never formally found.

According to Lasso he continued to haunt the vicinity long after his death and could not understand people's attitude towards him when they sensed his presence or by chance, when they saw him. Wasn't it, after all, his place? His family had moved away shortly after his death, the estate having been equally divided between his children who had sold the land in portions. Where Melina's house now stood (and which had been inherited from her parents) was once part of his estate. Many, many years had passed since his death and the estate was lost sight of. No one could remember having heard of any hauntings in the vicinity.

And all the time Lasso had wanted to return and had been rejected, as he put it, by other minds and bodies which he tried to invade. When asked where he had been all this time he replied that he had just 'been around' most of the time and that at other times he had been in situations he called indescribable because they were "out of this world". He couldn't fit in any place else. He didn't belong. He wanted to be back here, to master again the lives of others, to indulge in the type of living he once enjoyed. He didn't know who had murdered him or whether they

17

had ever met since his demise. He never saw his family. Only once did he come across the son with whom he had fought, but they soon parted company. He said that from time to time he saw some of his rich friends, who seemed to be very much in the situation he was in — neither believing nor trusting in anything beyond their riches — while on earth they were finding it difficult to settle in elsewhere.

All this narrative did not take place at once, it came out jerkily from time to time. One moment Lasso would appear relaxed, then suddenly becoming tense he would spit at them and rave. He didn't like wherever in hell he was (his own words) and was determined to return to the land of the living. He had sometimes babbled on and on as if he were trying verbally to free himself of his problems.

As the car neared Las Cuevas, Melina grew restless as if she, or the indwelling Lasso, knew that this was to be the final battle. She left the car clamped between Boyo and Lezama, their combined strengths only just enough to make this manageable. Her restlessness heightened as they neared the water's edge. Although she was no longer thrashing around there was still firm resistance, as though the thing knew that here, in water, would be its last stance — that here lay the determinative factor of its continued existence in Melina and that whatever the outcome it would be final. Fortunately the tide was in. They did not have to wade far out. After Mama Rose anointed Melina with her secret compound, which was perfumed, Melina was dunked incessantly, but left immersed only long enough to disturb the malevolent being who could not stay in its borrowed casing while it remained underwater. Mama Rose, backing the sea, was turned towards Melina and her escorts, while behind them was Marie Denise, fervently plying her rosary.

Loudly and vehemently Mama Rose commanded Lasso to leave Melina alone and to find some other habitation to which he might be more suited. Then the immersion was repeated successively. The thing named Lasso became en-

raged and the tigress-strength with which Melina was infused at times hindered her being pushed into the water.
At these times her voice coarsened and she belted back
vicious replies. Whatever Mama Rose said was immediately
repeated in chorus by Boyo, Lezama and Cousin Jojo who
had accompanied them into the water, so that it seemed
like one loud, multi-voiced echo of Mama Rose's phrases.
Nevertheless, Lasso answered back swiftly in between
dunkings. A chance onlooker would have imagined this
to be a rehearsed pantomime, with no prompters and none
of the cast losing his cue, for some of it went like this:

Lasso: "Go to Hell:

Mama Rose and Company: "You are the one who belong
in hell."

Lasso: "I will take her with me if I have to return."

Mama Rose and Company: "We will see that you go alone.
We know that you are uncomfortable. The body has been
anointed with holy oils. You must be uncomfortable. You
must leave now."

Lasso: (whining) "I want my estate back. I want to be here
again, to be a Hèffà — a boss. I want my mansion and
my servants ... and ... "

Before he was finished Melina was held down longer
than she had been so far, and on being brought up she
went limp, almost leaving the grip of the two men. Her
eyes remained closed. She shivered uncontrollably, then
completely relaxed. At the same time Marie-Denise fell
backwards into the water, as if she had been struck a swift
blow, and was helped to her feet by Jojo. She said later
that she felt herself being pushed out of the way though
she saw nothing. And this would seem to be the time when

19

Lasso, his resistance worn down by the hours of relentless effort on the part of Melina's friends, had departed.

When Melina was taken from the water, her thin dress clinging to her now wasted body, she was placed again in the backseat of the car and here, stripping off her wet garments, the women wrapped her in a blanket which had been *prepared* beforehand. For on this blanket, a few hours earlier, Ramon himself had lain — as envisioned by Mama Rose and Boyo. It was he who had instructed them as to the methods which would be most effective in ridding Melina of Lasso. To this blanket had been pinned the notation which had instructed that "The Lion of Juda had conquered — The Root of David". On this blanket had rested Ramon in order to infuse it with his own vibrations, which were contrary to those of the evil Lasso, and which Mama Rose had smoked beforehand with the aroma of sweet smelling herbs, crushed and burnt in the small brazier kept for such a purpose, and performing whatever other ceremony was appropriate to the occasion.

Lasso had left Melina's body. He would not be able to penetrate it again in order to reinstate himself, for precautions were being taken to keep him out. The blanket was a necessary step. The door which would lock him out permanently.

Melina was taken to Mama Rose's house. She would not be returned to her own home for a while yet. She was kept in a small room with the brazier constantly burning, emitting a sweet trail of frankincense tempered occasionally with the addition of dried herbs such as verte-ver. Melina steamed and sweated, and bore the discomfort of which at first, because of physical exhaustion, she was only dimly aware until, on the second day, she suddenly became, once again, her old self. She had been guarded, comforted, companioned and consoled throughout by Mama Rose, Boyo, and other willing helpers like Lezama and Marie-Denise. Soon Melina was smiling, telling them that she realised she had been ill and questioning the nature of her illness. At first they were reluctant to let her know the truth, but as time went by she learnt every detail, listened wide-eyed and wonderingly, for there was absolutely no recall, as there had been no awareness during those times.

Melina remained with Mama Rose for a few days until she was fully recovered and there was no longer any danger of Lasso reappearing on the scene, for he had taken himself off completely once he realised that the battle was lost.

Melina's home was cleansed by whatever simidimi Mama Rose thought necessary and Melina took up her abode there once more, and her life where it had temporarily halted.

*   *   *

Granpa would tell us the story of Damal and his sister some other time, he said, who no one had been able to help because the spirits which had invaded their bodies had been purposely *sent* by enemies of their parents. Therefore, Damal was doomed to mime at driving a motor car for the rest of his days; to travel on foot from Kalaruna to Mossdene, a distance of some twenty miles from north to south, and east to west of the island, always manoeuvering the imaginary steering wheel of his mentally-created motor car; while his sister would constantly turn the arm of a make-believe, manual sewing machine, and guide the pretend fabric along a non-existent presser foot. Someone like Mama Rose could not help them because she would first have to find out exactly what means were used by their parents' enemies to achieve this.

The spirit controls allowed them to eat and rest at the exact times they were used to doing these simple, human things. Though they seldom spoke, Damal would often shout at someone ahead, if his *horn* had not persuaded the careless *pedestrian* to get out of his way.

When approached, his sister would calmly answer un-voiced questions with the reply that she could not possibly accept any more work, as she was completely booked well ahead with a tremendous amount of dressmaking.

They were East Indians who lived in a small carat-roofed house of white-washed clay, in a remote district, where their father farmed the surrounding acre of fertile land. Damal and his sister Noonie, were already full-grown when disaster struck. Many professed that this injury had been done to them by someone holding a personal grudge against their father. The local Pundit had tried in vain to release them.

They had not been 'possessed' in the same way as Melina but, rather, obsessed — having been affected by the spirits' influences in such a way that they would be completely helpless mentally and physically, and be condemned to carry out the movements designated by the spirit-senders.

NOTE: These two characters actually existed in Trinidad, West Indies, for a number of years. Their real names have not been used. 'Damal' was cured of his hallucination some time before he died and became normal. It was difficult to learn any more about his sister. 'Damal' was seen by the author when she was a child, guiding his imaginary "car" through the streets of Port of Spain.

THE NIGHT OF THE SOUCOUYA

The only one who did not know about soucouyas was
Donald, and when Granpa said he would tell us a story
about a soucouya, he asked, "What is a soucouya?" ...
So Granpa had to explain all about "the one who sucks".
This was always thought to be an old woman with witch-
like qualities who shed her skin at night to become a ball
of flame and though wingless, could fly, entering houses
by mysterious means. Locked doors and windows were no
deterrent. The blood of others was necessary to their continued existence. It was surmised that this lengthened their
lives and kept them younger looking and more agile than
their natural years. Though they, too, succumbed to death
eventually.

"How it draw blood, Granpa?" Donald asked.

"Well ..." Granpa went on, "It would blow into yer
face while yer sleepin, make a hole in yer skin with its teeth
... after everybody else in the house was put to sleep
sounder, too, of course, and then ... and then ..."

The victim was usually a young person. The soucouya
would return again and again to the same victim, and if
this were allowed to continue indefinitely the victim could
become ill and die. It had been known that on occasion
a soucouya might discover that a potential victim's blood
held a very high salt content — children who liked eating
acid fruit with a pinch of salt to enhance its flavour, for
instance. This blood was anathema. Someone with a particular leaning towards salt, it was said, could make a
soucouya sick if it drew the blood before realising this.
Having discovered it at the first sampling she would never
return. A popular idiom was 'a soucouya would never suck
me. I eat too much salt'. There was no record of one ever
having been caught in the act, although there had been
legendary voicings of a discovery immediately after, when
the beholder screamed in fear and in horror, at the unex-
pected and unwelcome sight of the naked rawness of their

predatory visitor. Apparently this horrific being rose swiftly from the floor and shrunk to a size which accommodated its exit via the small air vent in one wall of the room, the windows being securely closed. As all the occupants of a house would first be put into a deep sleep, this was an isolated and presumably, exceptional incident caused by a late arrival at the house.

As we warmed to the narrative, Granpa recounted his personal experience with a soucouya.

* * *

It had been a good day at the races. Granpa's weakness, the horses, had brought him some twenty miles away from home to the small town of Aripana. He had been particularly lucky that day. Doubling on a 'forecast' his horses had come in just the way he had bought the doubles — Anaclevy and Handsome Brute, first and second, just as he had interpreted his dream. At a twenty-to-one payout on Anaclevy and seven-to-one on Handsome Brute his winnings were high. Having bought the doubles twice he had come off with winnings of over a hundred dollars, a good windfall. His friend James, who had accompanied him to the tracks, should help him celebrate. Not much of a drinker himself, Granpa nevertheless went with James to the nearest bar, where the day's bettings were revised, with James tossing off two shots to one of Granpa's from the Black Label rum bottle. The post mortem on the day's events was a pleasant one. They lost track of time and on arrival at the bus depot discovered that the last bus to Point Martin had left. The only alternative to spending the night on a park bench (there was no hotel) was hiring a car to take them home. They were both taking up work with the first shift next morning at six. If they slept in the park there would still be nothing available to get them to the oilfields by that time. They found a taxi driver who took pity on them and offered to get them home for a reasonable sum.

He was dropping a package off half-way to Point Martin anyway, he said, in Princess Town. No sooner had they settled down in the car than James fell asleep and Granpa was left to keep the driver company, with brief reminders of his friend's presence when James' head nodded heavily in his direction. So heavily in fact, that Granpa felt the impact each time it struck his shoulder. Some miles later the driver stopped.

"Ah ent going to be long. Just dropping this at the house over there." He indicated the half-seen light of a half-hidden house, secluded some yards away from the road and partly shielded by tall trees. He closed the door and lumbered away into the darkness with a large package which had been resting on the front seat beside him. Granpa made himself more comfortable, having gently pushed James' stocky frame into its own corner, and relaxed into a doze. He soon became aware that the driver had been gone longer than expected and wondered what time it was — perhaps going on eleven o'clock. In the heavy blackness of the wooded area it was difficult to tell. Country people retired early. It could be any time. His eyes were attracted to a light in the distance, to the right of where he sat, and his gaze lifted to the top of a tall tree where, silhouetted against the skyline, a bright glow hovered ... yes, hovered. It seemed to balance just above and beyond the treetop. Granpa recalled the last time he had observed something similar, but it was unbelievable that at such an early hour this could be happening, here, in a narrow dirt lane, the dim glow of a sheltered house light the only visible sign of life, apart from himself and James. He felt apprehensive. Watching closely he saw the light — an orange red ball — begin to spin, away from the tree and back to it, as if it were using the treetop as a gauge from which to pivot and return. Fascinated by the movement of the ball of light — more like fire it seemed. It held his gaze as it spun, moved away, returned, and seemed to hang from the tree at brief intervals. Granpa knew what it was.

He had seen it once as a young boy — a soucouya. He wished the driver would hurry back so they could get away from there.

"James ..." he called softly, patting James' shoulder. "Wake up, wake up, man ... something wrong ..." He felt annoyance towards the driver, who should have been back by that time.

"Look ..." Granpa pointed into the distance where the glow hovered. "Is a soucouya, James, a soucouya ... and so early ..." he added in wonderment.

James was suddenly alert. The light flashed off into the distance, revolving like a ball of flame which was spinning wildly around an axis. It circled and returned to its original position, hovering there.

The driver was returning to the car. He shot inside, slamming the door, and before Granpa or James could say anything he hurriedly started the engine.

"You fellars see what I see?" he asked breathlessly, turning the car around sharply and almost backing into a tree when he reversed to make the turn.

"This place is full of soucouyas yer know." He lit out at an unbelievable speed. James had barely caught sight of the fireball when they moved away and it was now lost to sight among the trees. The driver was telling them that he had seen it as he was leaving his friends' house. Knowing immediately what it was, he wanted to get away as fast as possible.

They talked about it all the way to Point Martin. Granpa's sixth sense told him that there was some connection between the object and one of the occupants of the car. At first he felt it was making its way to a nearby house, possibly the very house where the driver had gone. But he soon discarded the thought when James told him that his wife Noraleen, often felt that blood had been drawn from her at night. At such times, he said, there were black and blue marks on her body, usually her arms and legs, and she felt tired and listless for a couple of days after. The doctor once prescribed a tonic, saying she was anaemic, but he could not account for the bruises and Noraleen could never, at any such time, recall having had a blow, or bruising herself.

On hearing this the driver said, "Perhaps it's you it after." He repeated, "Perhaps they suckin you too and you don't know. After all yer was fast asleep." James could not accept this, taking umbrage at the suggestion.

But the driver's remark had set Granpa thinking. Was it possible that the soucouya had intended getting into the car at James? ... In which case it would have had to put him into a deeper sleep, and Granpa too. The idea was preposterous. And what of the driver? Did it know when he would return to the car? No one could remember a soucouya ever being caught in the act — this one could not have been that silly except, of course, it had ways or means of also mesmerizing the driver before he saw it. No! Their untimely presence had been discovered, that was all. Most likely it was now succeeding in its ghoulish plan in some nearby bedroom.

The driver, who they were now calling Ropey — after he had announced his name — Roman Lampey — and that he was known to his friends as Ropey, told James he knew an obeahman who would be able to help Noraleen put a stop to the blood-letting, if it were, in fact, the work of a soucouya. He gave James the address and said he would be willing to take him and his wife there, as it was some distance away, if they would contact him in advance. By this time they had arrived at Granpa's house. They had not seen the orange-red flame again, but Granpa felt relieved that his wife Thelma, was alright, as there had been a little nagging worry in his mind that the ball of fire concerned someone in the car. And if it were James (James' story ruled out Ropey) wasn't it possible it had gone on ahead of them to the compound, to the little two-bedroomed houses which they occupied as part of their benefits from the oil company? The incident of the sighting of the soucouya made Thelma uneasy. She was not normally a squeamish person. Her buxomness could be wielded quite usefully, if necessary, at a more tangible opponent.

Granpa made a mental note that he would remind James — sometime in the future, to take Noraleen to the obeahman before another blood-drawing session, just in case the precautions she had recently been advised to take, might fail. He, too, would like to visit the obeahman. He had never been to one and his curiosity was piqued.

"What is a obeahman?" This time the question was chorused by Robin, Zeta and me.

"He is ... well ... he's a sort of witch you might say ... yes ... a sort of witch, you see ..." And Granpa chortled softly, as though there was some secret joke that could not be shared. He continued, "He can do all sorts of things, good things and bad things. Well, I'll tell you about an obeahman another time, a voodoo man ... in some places he's a voodoo man."

He went on with the story, saying that on the following day a very agitated James told him that Noraleen's niece, Beryl, had arrived from Port of Spain while he himself was on his way home the previous night. She had been expected that weekend but they did not know on which day she would arrive. Tired from her trip she had turned in early. She was sharing the children's bedroom. Ronald, four, and Patsy just a year-old. Nora thought that she looked a bit peaked but of course, her long trip on an uncomfortable bus was undoubtedly the cause.

As he went into the kitchen for his breakfast that morning, James said, Noraleen was coming in from the backyard, looking concerned. She asked him to follow her and together they quietly entered the children's room. They were asleep. And so was Beryl, her young, shapely body lay motionless on the bed, the thin cotton sheet thrown to the floor, both her arms thrown back beside her head, palms up, and her nightdress was drawn half-way up one

28

thigh, where a hugh dark blotch marred the perfection of her smooth skin. Against the soft underskin of one up-turned arm two smaller bruises stood out. Nora pointed silently to the floor beside the bed and moved her finger along a dark trail of red spots leading to the door. None of the sleepers stirred. Noraleen and James followed the stains into the small dining room and through the backdoor to the yard. Here, in the brightness of the early morning, dark spots dotted the light dry soil and laid a trail to the guava tree a few yards away. Below the tree a small ex-cavation had showered upturned earth around its rim and here, where the trail of bloody spots ended, a massive pool of dark wetness had not yet seeped into the sod. The thick liquid, apparently discharged there in a hurry, told a story of hasty exit from the house and hastier offloading. The hole looked like that which could have been made by some animal — a dog perhaps, when it had chased some tiny quarry which had burrowed swiftly, and which could be followed only with its paws. But they knew this was not the case. Each pair of eyes held a question. James had said nothing about his experiences the night before, yet, in con-cert, their minds had arrived at the same conclusion. The work of a soucouya. This time it had struck gold. A more succulent victim than Nora — a young lithesome body. Never had the children been touched. Had it come to Nora and found Beryl instead? Or had it known of Beryl's pres-ence? She had visited from time to time but never with this effect. James then told his wife about the night's in-cident. She confessed that in the excitement of Beryl's ar-rival, and expecting him momentarily, she had forgotten to take the necessary precautions which had been advised by friends after her last encounter. She had not sprinkled salt around the doors and windows. She did not put a few grains of white rice on the windowsills and surround this with drops of asafoetida. No soucouya had gained entry since she had started doing this some months before. On the verge of tears she blamed herself, knowing that the children, too, had been left unprotected. They filled in the hole under the tree with earth and cleaned the spots in the house. Beryl and the children still slept. James was now determined to take the taxi driver's advice and see the obeahman.

Later that day James and Granpa discussed the situation and decided that the soucouya sighted the night before had traced James, knowing in some way that he was not at work and wanting to ensure there was time to do its dirtywork before he arrived at the house. They wondered if it had discovered Beryl's presence and its exercise had been solely to establish James' time of arrival at home and await his falling into a sound sleep. Surely no strange soucouya would know of Beryl's presence? Their immediate neighbours were all people who worked in the oilfields and their families, and they were the people most likely to know when he was on the night shift. If the soucouya they had seen was indeed the culprit, then it was someone who knew his whereabouts.

They could not establish exactly when the action had taken place, but judging from the congealed blood under the tree and apparently fresh spots in the house, it could not have been as distant in time as during his homeward journey. Furthermore, Nora had not been asleep — unless she had dozed without realising it. They concluded that it had occurred in the early morning. To be precise 'foreday morning'. But there was a change of tactic here. Never before had a soucouya entered the house during James' presence. Of course, the fact that Beryl slept in another room altered the circumstances. If it were the same soucouya they had seen miles away, then it had gone there to watch his movements, to gauge the time it would take him to get home. Perhaps it had means of discovering his whereabouts, remembering of course, that he had not arrived home on the late bus as expected. It was a chilling thought. Or perhaps it was the night of the soucouyas and they were all over the place.

James then told Granpa what he and Noraleen had heard prior to this: that the old woman who lived on the main road in a little two-roomed hut abutting a small shop, Miz Sarah, might be the culprit. She was a widow, but prefixing a woman's first name with Miss — pronounced Miz — was customary and it often remained this way all her life, regardless of the fact that she had got married. Because of Miz Sarah's weird, slightly eccentric appearance, she was often teased by children for whom she had little tolerance at the best of times. They called her 'a witch', taunting her from a distance so she would run after them. Some claimed she was a soucouya. She owned the largest wooden mortar ever seen. It was common knowledge that at nights a soucouya hid her temporarily discarded skin in a mortar. Many wished they had the courage to be out late at night, in order to search for the skin, when it could be salted and the soucouya would never be able to recover her raw flesh with it on returning from her night's excursion. They wanted to hear her call to it, using the chant of the soucouyas, the call of the skin:

> *Kin kin ah me kin*
> *ah me kin*
> *Kin kin ah me kin*
> *come to soucou*
> *come to soucou*

soothing it back to her raw body. 'Kin' instead of skin, the distortion no doubt a relic of African tongues mingling with the adopted English of their captive ancestry. They wanted to witness her squirm and panic, and try to hide her rawness when it would not return to her. Or to see her dance an uncontrollably diabolical dance in pain, and in anger, and in frustration, if it did return to her body in its pickled condition. It had been rumoured that some soucouyas had, in fact, replaced the salted skin only to suffer untold agonies. Unable to try this method of proof, the children contented themselves with scattering rice on her steps, in the hope that she would be caught redhanded in daylight, in all her rawness, painfully gathering the rice grains one by one, as they believed that she would not be able to move away until she had collected every grain, hoarding them in one hand. There were other known methods, but this was the most popular. Another method involved daubing the outside of her doors and windows with asafoetida, so that when she tried to enter she would become transfixed, and would stand there spellbound until daylight and until the scent had worn off. But Miz Sarah was a clever soucouya. No one had yet caught her.

James told Granpa that he and Noraleen had dismissed these rumours, though he recalled seeing her on a couple of occasions, while on his way to work very early in the morning, stooping outside her front door picking up the grains of rice that had been strewn there. She would be shuffling around and clucking, apparently gleaning some satisfaction from this, as she looked pleased, rather than annoyed. Once he had noticed a broom lying close at hand, and instinct hinted that no doubt she was about to sweep away the salt which would invariably have accompanied the rice.

On inquiring about Beryl next day, Granpa learned that she had not been well. She was listless. Noraleen had been feeding her eggnog and chicken broth to replenish the loss of blood. At first Noraleen and James agreed that as she seemed unaware of what had taken place she would not be told. She woke very late, could not understand why she had overslept as she was usually an early riser, and concluded that she was getting ill. This was unusual for she had always been a healthy, energetic girl and at nineteen could remember the exact amount of days in her life that she had been unwell.

Torn with indecision, Nora assumed that if Beryl learnt the reason for her supposed illness she would most likely be afraid to visit them again. On the other hand, Beryl did not mention the bruises. She was unaware that they had been discovered. Most likely she had not linked them to her sudden illness. They, in turn, never mentioned the trail of blood. Should they tell her that she was soucouya-prone in order that she could take some preventive measure in future? They asked Granpa's advice. No one could reconcile the fact of the blood being spilt. No one had ever heard of so much blood being returned afterwards. This had not been experienced on any of the occasions when Nora had been the victim. It was assumed, then, that there was some quality in Beryl's blood which was not conducive to a soucouya's digestion. Had it only been the excessive salt factor it would have ceased to draw immediately this was discovered. Drops of blood on the bedclothes or on the flooring was not unusual, especially if there was rejection, but in this case it had not only drawn, but had done so excessively, leaving Beryl very much depleted. There was no doubt that after having its fill the soucouya had hastily retreated to the tree base — had even begun to spill while still in the act — yet continued to gorge itself. And the question of *why* remained. It was not only the salt factor then, because this would have stopped it. There was something else. Some unknown quality in Beryl's blood which encouraged it to draw excessively yet became detrimental.

Granpa said she should be warned. She should be encouraged to find some means of protection like Noraleen had. If not the same soucouya, some other would most likely attack her again. They could not take her to the obeahman, as her parents might object, but they could find some solution and pass it on to her, for her own good.

On their first day off together from work Granpa accompanied James to the obeahman, Papa Weh Leh, in Bushajou. Ropey took them in his car. Beryl had long since returned to her home, a little wiser in the ways of thwarting soucouyas. Noraleen and James were not sure whether she believed what they had told her. Nora, especially, had been puzzled by her reaction or, rather, lack of reaction. For though she smiled shyly when told, and seemed to accept their story, nevertheless, she turned away as if she were ashamed and for the rest of her stay was unusually quiet and withdrawn. I was left with the impression that Granpa had some other explanation for all this, but would not say it. I could tell from his chuckle!

The obeahman confirmed that what Noraleen was doing was effective and advised that she should continue. The soucouya had entered the house because she had omitted to safeguard it that particular night. He also advised that for a small charge he could provide greater protection for her and the children — and James too, if he were so minded, in the form of a tiny, sealed, cloth sack to be worn near the body. The ingredients, he said, were potent enough to ward off more than just soucouyas, and they need never concern themselves again if they each possessed one. For an additional sum he could pinpoint the culprit and put her out of commission for good. He himself had no love for soucouyas. If James could not afford the small fee, he said, tongue in cheek, a couple of chickens or whatever livestock his wife was prepared to part with, would be welcomed. James confessed to Granpa afterwards that he suspected Papa Weh Leh had overheard him discussing the vegetable garden in which Nora took such pride and the few chickens they kept.

The obeahman offered to take care of the guilty soucouya personally. He refused to tell them who it was, although he professed to know. When he closed his eyes, he said, he could see her plainly. He gave no description, and agreed it was the same soucouya they had seen on the way home that night. He mentioned that once he told someone who it was, giving them a definite description, and the party, being impatient, had gone straight to the suspected soucouya and had beaten her up, getting into trouble with the law and naming *him* as their advisor. The fact that they had ill-treated someone who was innocent of any wrongdoing made matters no better. Since then, he said, he kept his own council, and his methods of operation were mystical ones. He had his owns corps of helpers who would go where they were instructed to carry out his wishes. Advising them to be patient he said it would take two or three weeks to finalize matters.

James tried to trick him into saying if it was Miz Sarah. It seemed that, despite his denials, James had decided that it was her. There was no one else in the vicinity who fitted so well into the framework of a soucouya. By the time he had gone to the obeahman it was a foregone thing. But Papa Weh Leh remained silent. All he would say further on the matter was that the soucouya which had attacked Beryl had been hovering nearby while James was on his way home, tracing his progress in order to be sure that he, too, would be sound asleep when it came. He also told them that Beryl's blood had been pure, and sweet, encouraging the evil one to gorge herself, but he could give no explanation as to why it had vomited.

* * *

Some weeks later:

It is early morning and Thelma is waking Granpa by shaking him roughly:

"Wake up, Felix, wake up ..." she hisses frantically "I hear somebody bawlin ..."

Sleepily-conscious Granpa listens, and in the distance, tempered by the raucous crowing of cocks, he hears a terrifying scream, followed by what must be a desperately loud moan.

Granpa rises, dresses hurriedly, and as he steps outside intending to satisfy his curiosity as to where the sounds are coming from, he sees one of the workmen who lives next door hurrying in his direction:

"I dunno what happen, Felix, but I think somebody in serious trouble ... that screechin coming from Jerry

Thomason house," the man says.

They hurry off together in the direction of Jerry Thomason's house two doors away. The backdoor is open and without ceremony they enter, assuming that the cause of the now louder cries permits this license. Jerry's wife, Margaret, stands in the kitchen, horror transfiguring her heart-shaped, chocolate brown face into a puzzled frightened mask. Speechlessly she points in the direction of a small bedroom. They go towards it and through the opened door they see Jerry, astonished and quite bewildered, staring at his old aunt Betsy, who is naked, her hands held before her in an endeavour to hide her privateness. Her skin looks rough and raw as if it has been turned inside out ... blistered ... disguising her age-old creases. Such a terrible sight has never been experienced by any of them. They have never seen someone who appears to be completely burnt — for this is what they think has happened. She cries out incoherently. Only a few words can be snatched from the mass of gibberish. "My skin ... burnin ... burnin ..."

Jerry throws a sheet around her. Whatever cooking oils and other emollients can be gathered are used to anoint her. She cannot lie down but paces restlessly, crying and moaning until she is completely anointed, the oil being poured straight from the bottle to her aching body runs down to the floor where blobs of oiliness intersect the clean, scrubbed boards.

Jerry's wife comes into the room and as her gaze rests on a large opened can of greenish looking cream on the dressing table she reaches out to take it up, no doubt thinking it could be of use. Aunt Betsy sees her, realizes her intention, and with a swift movement knocks the jar out of Margaret's hand, scrambling after it on the floor to throw it under the bed. Astonished beyond comprehension no one stops her. Jerry reaches for the large blue lid, intending perhaps to read what is inscribed on it, but she does the same thing, grabbing and throwing it after the jar.

Later she lay on soft cotton padding with only a thin cotton coverlet over her and stayed this way for days until, with the soothing effect of the oils, she was able to get around once more. Granpa seemed the only one with whom she was willing to talk, although he was far younger than she was. He remained with her and he was given an explanation which he would not reveal to anyone, as she had requested. She staunchly refused to see a doctor. Granpa visited each day until she was better, drawing from the store of useful knowledge he had acquired over the years, and advising her of which herbs, because of their healing qualities, should be used when she took her regular 'bush bath'.

Everyone stayed away from her, fearing contagion, as the description of her illness prompted, in some minds, thoughts of 'shingles'. Eventually, the mystery of her sudden illness became a story which grew myriad limbs — becoming a tree well-nourished in the soil of superstition.

James had been told by the obeahman that he should return to see him within three weeks of his first visit. By that time, the man had said, he would have been able to locate the soucouya and, in his own way, to have conquered her. When James, conversationally, brought him up to date on the recent incident of Aunt Betsy he smiled cunningly, clucked, shook his head wisely, and ventured the remark that he, personally, knew there was at least one soucouya who would never bother anyone again, not revealing to James, of course, what, if anything, he had done to ensure this. He let drop hints to the effect that his intervention created a more damaging effect to the activities of the soucouya concerned than to her body — so that the physical discomfort would only be temporary, while the hindrance to her devilry would be lasting. Neither would he venture name, nor description of the alleged soucouya.

Granpa ended his story here and our questions were flashed at him faster than the forthcoming replies. Was it

Aunt Betsy? What was the cream for — did anyone ever find it? What was it she had said to him which he couldn't tell? Granpa replied that as he had promised secrecy he still could not reveal it. And Donald, asking stupidly if Miz Sarah was a soucouya why did Aunt Betsy's skin get blistered?

"Did she use that cream to take her skin off?" Rita asked.

He shook his head negatively, but still did not reply, only chuckled, one of his deep meaningful chuckles which by now I had come to know so well. Then he mumbled, absentmindedly, that those who would not grow old gracefully but tried, through man-made elixirs, to find eternal youth — denied by the Fates who were wiser — were likely to court disaster.

I sat in deep thought afterwards, not listening completely to some of the fragmented questions the others were asking, my mind returning to Miz Sarah, and somewhere from the very depths of my being surfaced the knowledge that I did not want to become old, and poor, and ragged, for it would seem that these were the signs by which one were recognized as a soucouya.

THE JUMBIES

Martha looked at the coffee dregs in the old enamel pot and shook her head solemnly from side to side. A faint sigh escaped her, but went unnoticed, because Martha had sighed so often lately it had begun to be accepted as second nature — at least by herself. She poured boiling water over the dregs — yesterday's leftovers, because on alternate days they had fresh coffee, and the dregs were used on the following day to eke out the week's purchase as long as was humanely possible. The children didn't seem to mind the difference. But she did. Out of a life of constant denial, the one thing she missed more than anything else was a good cup of coffee. All her life had been spent in between pennies. When the pennies were there they existed. When they were not, she waited patiently for the time when they would be. If things had been bad before — and there were times when they had been very bad — since Damion's death they had become far worse.

She placed the pot on the coal fire, stirred it, and waited for the water to bubble before taking it off — this way they got more of the flavour out of the dregs — heaven knows it had been weak enough the day before. Tomorrow they would have to drink bush tea. Perhaps mint, or shining bush. There wasn't much coffee left and she saw no way of buying more before the end of the month.

As she sliced the remainder of yesterday's bake for breakfast she thought of how things had gone since the day when Damion and his friend Mervyn, who was Evelyn's godfather, had not returned, and their boat — Mervyn's boat it was really, but he shared it with Damion who never could manage to get himself one — was found overturned on the reef where it had been washed up. Their bodies were never found.

When the fish had been coming in, the pennies were also. Now, with Damion's death, and only the meagre wage she got from working as a daily maid with one of the white families in St. Clair, only God knew how she would continue to manage. He would also know, she hoped, how she would manage to guide and train their four children. Evelyn, going on thirteen, reserved, as always, not giving the trouble at which Denise, ten, was apt. She didn't know where Denise got her temper and fiery personality from. And Jimmy. He was the real problem. That boychild was going to be the death of her. At eight he had the knowledge, the cunning and the uncontrollability of both girls, plus his father's attitude towards life. Damion had been a dreamer. So was Jimmy. At his birth no father was prouder than Damion. This was *the one*. This was the child who would raise his nose in his old age. This was the boy who would have everything, and do all *he* never could. Jimmy was four when Carl came. It wasn't too bad Carl being a cripple. Because they had Jimmy. But it had been Carl who missed Damion most. He had pined, getting thinner and thinner as he watched and waited for his father — unable to understand that he would never come again. Martha had never tried to explain. She couldn't.

If Damion had been out at sea all night, he would go straight to the crib when he got in, in the early morning, to see if Carl was awake and to take him up and play with him if he were. If he came in during the late afternoon, Carl would spend part of the evening on his lap ... or Damion would tickle him, pull his ears, play with him on the floor. At these times, listening to Carl's laughter, they forgot that he could not and would never walk. They forgot, until they looked at him, that one arm was withered and useless. It had taken Carl a long time to talk, but now, at last, he was beginning to do so hesitantly but nevertheless, quite clearly. As Martha stripped a piece of saltfish, she wondered what she had done to deserve such a fate — perhaps she had been bad in another life. Some people believed in reincarnation; perhaps once she had done terrible things for which she was now paying. If not, perhaps there would be a next life ahead, when things would be far better. There was no way of accounting for the blows life had dealt and was still dealing her. She wondered how long she would bear up alone under the strain. In the year since Damion's death the neighbours had been very kind. But they, too, needed all they had. After the initial shock of bereavement she realized that soon the loaves of bread, the odd bottle of coconut oil, the dollar thrust in her hand, would cease. As she bustled about getting some 'pap' for Carl — who refused to eat saltfish no matter how hungry he was, she also thought of how she would have to stay up late that night finishing Denise's dress for the Corpus Christi procession next day. But now she must hurry or she would be late for work. There was no time to comb her hair. She passed one work-worn hand over head, feeling the mass of coarse black hair not yet tinged with any sign of grey. Once she was considered petite. Now, four children and many hard years later, she was almost dumpy. The hair which was once well-kept and had proudly framed her small, round face, was often unkempt. She would tie her head when she got to work. This way she would not have to spend precious time combing it; that could be done later. In the meantime her old straw hat would hide it.

"Mo..ooo..om." Martha knew who it was without turning around. Only Jimmy spoke like that.

"Mooom, I want a penny to buy a lead pencil. I lost mine. I think somebody in school steal it." As Martha looked at her son she knew it would never dawn on him to ask for a cent pencil. He had explained to her before that they were no good, the lead was too soft. He wanted a penny one which was better. Evelyn and Denise always managed, somehow, with a cent pencil.

"I ent have a cent to spare today, fer a pencil or anything else. Ask yer teacher to lend yer one until tomorrow. Tomorrow you'll get a penny." Martha had no idea where the penny would come from on the next day, but she was thinking of asking Mr. O'Laughlin to lend her three dollars until the end of the month, just a week away, when it

41

could be deducted from her pay.

"Ah'll tief back one ..."

Jimmy's grouching startled her as she watched him settling himself at the old pitch pine table.

"You do that, and ah'll fix yer behine so yer doh sidong fer a week."

She knew that Jimmy would carry out his threat. Problems with him were on the increase faster than she could cope. And on top of it all was that *other* thing, the jumbie she had been seeing and which, on one occasion, Jimmy, too, had seen.

One night, months before Damion's death, while alone in the small detached kitchen fixing supper, through the back window she saw a man walking towards the house. In the darkness she could not see clearly what he looked like. He continued to approach, then, as he neared the kitchen and was just a few feet away, he disappeared. Martha had stood hesitantly for a few seconds, then she had walked to the kitchen door, looked up and down, walked around to the side and looked as far as she could see in every direction along the expanse of their large, bare backyard, bordered by a mass of trees. Nothing! Yet she was as sure that she had seen a man, as she was sure she had seen her husband a few minutes earlier in his blue dungaree shirt.

She said nothing about the incident to anyone, until a few weeks later when she saw him again. As before, he was dressed in what appeared to be a white shirt and, indistinctly, khaki pants. This time he stood outside the backdoor of the house, like a waiting sentinel, still and silent, and as she focussed on him, again without getting a distinct idea of his features, he disappeared. Martha felt she should have been afraid. But for some inexplicable reason she wasn't. She had sensed nothing evil about the spirit — for this is what it was, a Jumbie. This time she told Damion and his only comment, at first, was that she was 'seein jumbie'. Eventually he suggested she should tell

Ma Ellen about it. Ma Ellen would be able to advise them. She was very old. She had had experiences of all kinds and knew what would be most effective as a protective measure if it were necessary.

Ma Ellen came to the house one late afternoon, walked about the yard and the kitchen, said she sensed a presence at times, but that it was nothing evil. Perhaps just some deceased relative paying them a visit, or a friend who was now forgotten but who had not forgotten them. Ma Ellen advised her just to pray for God's protection for herself and her family. That was all there was to it! What had bothered Martha and Damion at first, was the insecurity of not knowing whether it was a good or a bad jumbie. Bad jumbies could bring you the worst possible luck; perhaps that was why things had not gone well for them. On the other hand, a good jumbie could also influence your surroundings and help to protect you. Somehow Martha felt, and confirmed this to Damion, that it was not evil. All she asked was that it would rest in peace.

Others had seen jumbies either in the day or at night. Time was immaterial although, of course, the night provided shade for the sons of the devil and these would choose that particular time for their wanderings, more so than in the daytime.

Then one morning, Jimmy mentioned that he had seen a man standing at the opened front door. Jimmy had approached and greeted him, intending to inquire whether he wanted to see one of his parents. Instead of answering, the man had disappeared. Jimmy immediately told them about it. All Damion had said was 'yer seein jumbie'. But Martha had told Jimmy that perhaps he had imagined it and there had been no one there. She didn't know what else to tell him, having kept her own experience from the children.

Furthermore, she had told him not to keep saying he had seen things which were not there. Jimmy never mentioned again whether he had seen the jumbie-apparition.

Martha remembered that her own father — God rest his soul — had told them over and over again the story of when he was a younger man working on the night shift at the pumping station, and going home on one occasion about two in the morning. He suddenly saw ahead of him an extremely tall man dressed in dark clothes, standing in the middle of the road — so tall he could not see his face. As he continued walking towards him the man grew to an enormous height and spread his long legs apart, spanning the roadway. But there was sufficient space between his legs for the tallest man to walk through. Martha's father felt afraid. He realized he was seeing a jumbie. He stopped walking, uncertain of what to do. By this time it was necessary to look way up into the air to see the man's body. His head had disappeared into space. Afraid to turn back, in case the jumbie followed, Martha's father squatted on the side of the road, his legs crossed one over the other and his arms folded, waiting for the jumbie to make whatever move it intended. It disappeared. Rising to continue on his way, Martha's father noticed that the man — or jumbie — had re-appeared in the opposite direction just a few yards away, along the road which he himself had just passed, and there began to stretch itself again. The road ahead now clear he continued on his way, walking as fast as he could, not daring to look back, and fearing that if he did do he may suffer some physical damage. He had heard this was what happened if you looked back at a jumbie. Unless you had the good sense to look over your left shoulder with your legs crossed, or bend over and look through your own legs at it. Whatever the method he was not interested. He only wanted to get out of its way, fearing it would materialize ahead of him again.

Martha had remembered this all her life especially on carnival days when she saw a 'Moko Jumbie' — a masquerader on very high stilts — a mock-up of a jumbie.

Now, filling the children's cups with the weak, sweetened coffee, she wondered what kind of jumbie had attached itself to them. After a lapse of many weeks she had seen it again the day before.

No use thinking about it now, she must hurry. She wanted to leave work a bit earlier that afternoon as she yet had to finish Denise's dress for the Corpus Christi procession on the following day — the Feast of Corpus Christi.

Martha feels a sense of pride as she stands waiting on Marine Square (now Independence Square) to see her children go by in the procession. She stands on the North Side, on the square itself, flanked by a hoard of others who have come to watch and who also fill the sidewalk on the opposite side. She had worked hard to finish Denise's white cotton dress — the dress Denise almost didn't get if her neighbour June Sandy, had not given Martha the three yards of cotton she had at home, in exchange for Denise's First Communion dress which she had long outgrown.

Martha had sat up late the previous night, painstakingly adding tiny tucks to the front of the blouse, edging the sleeves and collar with the narrow white lace she had been hoarding for such an occasion. Fortunately, Evelyn was wearing her Girl Guides uniform.

The procession snakes itself around the corner. The huge cathedral in the background is hungrily hugging a mass of celebrants in its forecourt who are milling forward as one body into the street, to lose itself in the winding trail ahead. High in the air, the clock face on its Norman facade indicates that it is ten o'clock. The procession is headed by a replica of the Virgin Mary, borne along at shoulder height on a rose-covered bier by four stalwart bearers. The Holy Mother, soft features and benign, stands commandingly erect. Priests and acolytes follow, a brass crucifix held high, a brazier, seemingly cold, dangles resignedly from the tapering fingers of a youthful acolyte.

Denise who somehow always manages to be at the forefront of events at school, is one of the flower girls. She holds a trailing white ribbon at the lefthand rear corner of the bier. Her crown of white organdy flowers adds an almost angelic touch to her small dark face, contradicting an impish reflection there. Her eyes dart swiftly from one side of the square to the other. She does not see her mother. But Martha's heart swells with pride at the green promise flickering around the edges of her tiny budding flower.

And Jimmy! Martha didn't particularly want to see him. At that moment he represented annoyance. An annoyance provoked some hours earlier when he had been sent with a dollar — part of the money borrowed from her employer, to buy two small sweetbreads (which would be cut in halves: it was Corpus Christi and the children needed a little treat) a breadfruit from an old woman with a tray outside the parlour, and a piece of saltmeat from the *Chinee* shop, which would be open for only a short while as it was a holiday. But what did he do? He bought the sweetbreads and the saltmeat. But no breadfruit. Instead he had paid a shilling for a sweepstake ticket from the vendor who often hawked the Turf Club tickets on the Main Road. Disappointment and frustration had caused Martha to react harsher than usual. Twenty-four cents gambled away when there were bus fares to be paid so they could get to the city — four cents for herself and a penny for each child, either way, excluding Carl who was left with the neighbour who looked after him when Martha was at work. A whole shilling gambled away uselessly. Jimmy's excuse had been that he and Denise didn't like breadfruit, only Evelyn. No thought of what they would have for lunch on return. Martha shuddered with renewed irritation as she remembered tearing the ticket in two and throwing it on the floor, from where Evelyn had retrieved it. "That Jimmy will be the death of me," she said softly to herself.

Jimmy's school is passing. Jimmy spots his mother. A broad grin intensifies the slant of his lips. The morning's episode forgotten he grins at her broadly, engagingly. She returns his smile and strengthens acknowledgment with a wave. He is gone and she is left with the image of herself snatching the sweepstake ticket from his hands and tear-ing it in two, throwing the two halves at him and watching them flutter helplessly to the ground. Evelyn had picked them up.

Remorse straddles Martha's thinking as she tries to con-centrate on the 'Children of Mary', the Sunday School group now approaching. Their white dresses gleam in the sunshine, their crowns and veils an emblem of the purity and holiness of youth and their dedication to the Holy Mother. The boys are wearing short blue serge pants and white long-sleeved shirts each sporting a tiny ribbon-hung medallion on its left breast, proclaiming the wearer's af-finity with and symbolic reverence towards the Mother of Divinity. Martha's attention is arrested by the glint of sun-shine caught and held momentarily by some of the medallions.

A blue silk banner inscribed 'St. Vincent de Paul Society' in gold lettering saunters past, held at a rakish angle.

Two companies of boy scouts follow.

Keenly Martha watches the Red Cross nurses who come next, wondering if Evelyn or Denise would one day become a nurse, or perhaps just a member of the Red Cross and wear a white uniform with a red cross on the apron bib. She would like that, to see her girls looking starched and proud. Starch ... they didn't have any starch ... or cof-fee either for that matter. Twenty-four cents could have bought a penny starch, with fifteen cents for coffee ...

Remorse proclaims itself. Martha feels guilt. Poor child! She must stop being so bitter! The end of the procession approaches. Others who attended the mass as individuals and not attached to any specific group make up the rear. A conglomeration of species: black, white, baccra, chinee, coolie, all types. Mulattoes, brown skins, some well dressed, some shabbily so, others in-between. The new middle class — the well off. The deprived and, perhaps, among them, the depraved. They are all here. The photographer from the only daily newspaper. Some private ones, among whom are tourists.

But the jumbie ... could anybody take a photo of a jumbie? Martha ponders.

A few days later when Martha came from work Jimmy was not at home. She inquired about him. Evelyn said that he had come in from school, as usual, had had some pap, then ran back out without saying where he was going. This had been nearly an hour before. Martha said nothing. When Jimmy returned she expected a sound excuse for his behaviour. *Her* children were not used to running off without good reason. That boychild was going to be the end of her. She would try to control her temper when he came back.

Jimmy ran straight into the kitchen. He was breathlessly trying to say something. A newspaper was clutched under one arm. A piece of dirty whiteness fluttered from a closed palm. He had difficulty catching his breath:

"Mama ... look ..." He shoved a piece of tattered paper towards her. He said Mama, not moom, not cajolingly, something serious was afoot. She looked at the piece of paper held between his fingers. The numbers written on it meant nothing to her. She saw only five or six digits scrawled crazily across a piece of crumpled copybook page.

"The sweepstake ..." It was Evelyn who had spoken. She left the kitchen immediately and Jimmy, now less excited and breathless explained why he had run off. On his way from school, he had seen the billboard outside the parlour which stated that the sweepstake numbers had been drawn and were published in the daily papers. They never bought newspapers. Sometimes on Sundays he would be sent over to June Sandy's to borrow theirs for his mother. Anyway, he decided to check the number on their ticket, which had been stuck together with flour and water, by Evelyn. This was the number on the piece of paper he held. Having done this he had run over to the Sandy's house and found Mr. Sandy reading the papers. He waited until he was finished to borrow it. This was the reason he had been delayed in getting back. On checking the newspaper he had found that their number was included in the draw.

Evelyn returned with the patched-up ticket. The newspaper was spread out on the table, which was specially cleared, and everyone checked it himself, to verify that everyone else was right. There it was. *Their* number — the ticket Jimmy had bought — 24916. The ticket was almost as good as whole; the figures printed opposite their number showed that the holder of the ticket would receive $10,000. Not first, but second prize, yet, a fortune. Denise was jumping up and down in the middle of the small room. Now she could get a bicycle, a ladies Raleigh, which she always wanted. Now she could get it. She jumped into the air, arms upraised in a wildly fiendish ballet. She twirled, clapped her hands and tapped her feet in erratic steps. Evelyn, beaming as if she had been awarded the last smile on earth, quietly stated that she would like a leather school bag, so that she would no longer have to carry her books on her arms, not 'tote' them, she said.

Martha was too stunned to react. She sat down at the table, looking bewilderedly at the ticket resting on the opened newspaper, unable to assess her own transport from a quiet rage against Jimmy to this ... this uncertain feeling of not knowing whether to be elated, because elation had been divorced from her life for such a long time she was not sure whether she could suddenly become acquainted with it again.

Jimmy was playing with Carl. He was sharing the news with him. Carl, who would not yet understand what this meant in their lives. Jimmy's voice, as he laughed and talked to Carl, arrested her attention. He was saying that they could now buy a chair with wheels so Carl could be pushed about. Carl's infant laughter echoed through the kitchen as Jimmy tickled under his chin. Martha couldn't believe her ears. That boychild of hers was going to raise her nose after all. She hoped Damion would know about it. Right now she needed a cup of coffee. Martha rose and walked unsteadily to the shelf where the coffeepot stood. As she reached up to take it down Evelyn's voice grated disharmoniously against the jubilation she was gradually working up.

"Mama ... look ... the serial number."

Martha returned to the table to see Evelyn pointing to the ticket, then to the printed numbers. It took her a while to follow what Evelyn was trying to say. The number was the same, but not the serialized letter. Their ticket number was preceded by the letter 'J'. The ticket drawn, the same as theirs, carried the letter 'I'.

"But ... we have the same number ..." Martha said lamely.

"But not the same letter," Evelyn replied.

Martha sat heavily on the chair with the feeble legs, leaning on the table to support herself. This was too much.

"But that was the one he wanted me ... to take ..." Jimmy's voice piped in uncertainty. "He smiled when I picked that one ..."

"Who wanted you to take it?" Martha asked.

"Well ..." Jimmy hung his head shyly. It was the first time in years since Martha had seen him look abashed.

"The man ... the jumbie," his voice was almost inaudible as he raised his eyes to his mother's face and saw the perplexity there.

"What jumbie ...?"

"Disconcertedly, Jimmy explained that he had been seeing the man regularly — the man his mother called a jumbie. To Jimmy he was just another man, like anyone else, except that he disappeared after you had seen him. The first time this happened he had been told that it was his imagination, so he kept quiet about it when he saw the man time and time again, especially as he always smiled at him in a friendly way. The day he bought the ticket he had seen the man when he was leaving the parlour. The man indicated, by pointing that he should buy a ticket. Jimmy said he went up to the hawker, who was holding out two books, looked at the tickets in both, then as he looked up at the man, who had moved closer to him as if he, too, wanted to see the tickets, the man smiled and bowed his head. Jimmy bought the ticket which he *thought* the man had smiled about. Now, as he spoke to his mother, suddenly he had doubts, realizing that, after all, the man may have been smiling because he had just touched a ticket in the seller's *other hand* — in the I series, he thought. Perhaps in the I series ... he wasn't sure now ... he was becoming confused.

"You still seein that man ... that jumbie?" Martha whispered.

Jimmy said he had not seen him since buying the ticket. Before this he had only seen him from time to time.

Evelyn was still looking at the papers, reading the printed lines below the listing. She cried out, handing the newspaper to her mother. "Look ..." she said excitedly, and Martha read that tickets in other series, but with the identical numbers as the listed ones would receive consolation prizes. She read the rest avidly, concluding that their ticket was worth, according to what the papers stated: $4,000. Thank God! That was still a fortune. And to think, to think, that it was the jumbie who had instigated all this. A *good* jumbie.

Feeling it was all too much for her, Martha rose and again walked to the coffeepot. Whatever it was, whether it was ten dollars or ten hundred dollars, she was still bewildered. She bustled about raking the hot coals together in the coalpot, blocking out from her ears the din which was going on. Blocking out Denise's demands which included, somewhere, a bicycle, and Carl's laughter.

Evelyn had been reading the fine print on the reverse of the ticket. As Martha placed the pan of water on the fire, Evelyn said, in a loud, distorted voice, "It marked here, that if the ticket mu..mut..il..aated, no money going to be pay out."

She looked helplessly at her mother who, she realized,

had not heard a word of what she was saying.

Martha was gingerly spooning coffee into the pot, carefully measuring the remainder in the 'sweetie' tin with a practiced eye. Then, as if on second thoughts, she lifted the tin and the rest of the coffee — a good heaping spoonful — slid joyfully into the pot. Martha was unaware that she was smiling, or unaware of what Evelyn had said.

Granpa could not remember if Martha had been allowed a consolation prize on their ticket.

THE NIGHTS OF LA GAHOOS

Granpa's own personal experiences were no less thrilling. In fact, they were more so because he had been born with the 'Caul' over his face and anyone born with the Caul was not only a 'seer', endowed with the power of supernatural vision, but was protected against evil spirits. Furthermore, he was born feet first, walking out into the world as it were, instead of crowning. This too put him into a privileged position. Spirits and other elementals which remained invisible to most people were apparent to him. He could not be harmed by them because he had walked out into the world. He had been born with wisdom not imparted to the average man or woman.

Some of his experiences were hair-raising. And because they were Granpa's, to us they were special. Knowing since childhood that he was born with the Caul he had learnt not to be afraid of anything — like meeting with La Gahoos. His first experience of them shook him up a bit, that was all, it just shook him. Not that he was afraid. It was just that he wasn't sure whether they were humans who had taken the forms of animals — werewolfs, or whether they were evil spirits who were known to wander on earth at unearthly times in animal form.

The La Gahoos, although in some ways the male counterpart of La Jablesse, differed in that whereas some of them were disembodied spirits taking the form of a human male with a cleft foot. (They were always male, but as women were never out late at nights unescorted they could not lure them away like La Jablesse — though they had been seen by women who were on their way to church at around four-thirty in the morning, when it was still dark, in time for the first mass at five o'clock, or by vendors on their way to the markets.) They also took the complete animal form at times, especially the human la gahoos, people who had dealings with the devil and who perhaps, had sold their souls to him for material gain. They changed their bodies at night into that of animals and wandered freely through the dark, quiet neighbourhoods, often just for the sake of changing, in order to prove their powers, through satanic endowment, over mere humans. Or perhaps it was the price demanded by Satan in order to seal their allegiance.

Sometimes one would roam quietly, appearing and disappearing to those who saw it, until they realized they were witnessing a supernatural phenomenon. Others were more disturbing, like the Belmont Donkey which roamed through the streets, especially through Bell Eau Road, frightening people until no one wanted to be on that street late at nights.

It would run up and down, then stand still and blow flames through its nostrils, pursuing those who ran from it. It was rumoured that one man had had a heart attack after being pursued by the Belmont Donkey. He burst into his house, told his wife what he had seen and collapsed. No one knew what put a stop to it, but locals thought that as it had claimed a victim its purpose had been served and it could now go to its rest; or perhaps appear in some other part of the world as another animal, doing the same thing. Anyway, whatever it was that had caused it to cease appearing was effective, because it stopped as suddenly as it had started and its remembrance was soon filed away in the archives of time.

One night Granpa was returning home after playing cards with friends about two miles from where he lived. He had been warned that as it was Hallowe'en he should not be abroad alone so late — it was about 1:00 a.m. His friends advised him to remain at their home until morning. "There are worse than witches afoot," they said, "on such a night."

Granpa did not own a donkey or a bicycle, and few cars were available. It was not unusual then, to walk home at all hours, if you did not wish to remain with friends. Whistling to wile away the time he walked briskly. There was no moon but it was one of those bright, clear nights when, except for shadows cast by underbrush and trees, one could see a little way ahead. He was used to walking here and as a matter of course, he was day dreaming — or night dreaming — when he heard a sound behind him. Looking back he soon recognized the huge dog which was now almost abreast of him.

It was the Doberman owned by people who lived nearby, or so he thought, but on its back was a small animal, an Agouti. Incredible! The dog and the agouti — the small wild animal often hunted by dogs — are deadly enemies. A dog never passes up an opportunity to hunt an agouti when the scent crosses its trail. And in the dead of night a dog with an agouti poised comfortably on its back loping past, was enough to convince any teetotaller that he was hopelessly drunk. It took a while to clear his mind of the incredible picture. No one would believe him if he said this. No one could possibly believe that a man who was not drunk could think he had seen such a sight. And he was not drunk! Of that he was absolutely sure! And he had seen them clearly ... had watched as they went past and out of sight. Still thinking of this he heard in the distance ahead the sound of approaching hooves, the clippity clop of what must either be a mule, donkey or horse. 'At this time of night' he wondered. This time he became wary ... the hairs on his back and chest felt as if they were raised ... he had not experienced this before but he did now. Slipping behind a low hibiscus fence he crouched, watching to see what came by. A mule passed. It walked leisurely. Not cropping the grass on the side of the road as it would usually do if it had strayed out of its compound, or if its tether had become loosened and it had walked away from its master's place. Not cantering, just going by slowly and ensconced behind the bush, Granpa, peering out through an opening in the leaves, saw that around its middle was coiled a huge snake, the head upraised behind that of the mule's, swirling gracefully. He would not have known that it was a snake coiled around the mule if it had not been for the head, larger that any snake's head he had ever seen, almost as large as a man's. He didn't know what kind of snake it was, a boa constrictor perhaps? But not with such a huge head! What then? And wrapped around the mule ... not hurting it, just wrapped around ... its head moving rhythmically as if it were timing the beat of the mule's hooves. Two deadly enemies again ... the snake and the mule. A mule would shy away from the slightest movement which resembled that of a snake's. And here in the dead of night, he had seen this. A mule would never allow a snake to become wrapped around it like that. It would bolt at the scent of one. It would try to trample it. It would bray. It would run away. But he had seen this with his own eyes. He knew now forsure that he had witnessed two spectacles which were not of this world. First a dog with an agouti on its back. And now this. There was no doubt in his mind but that they were the same creatures in different forms. He swore he would never be out again so late, and alone. Not that he was afraid. Granpa wasn't afraid, it was only that he realized the night was for the ungodly, and humans should be indoors. Only heaven knew what he would encounter next, he thought, as he resumed walking. Shortly afterwards he again heard the canter of hooves and again he ducked behind a low fence. This time a donkey came by, grey and shadowy. A large snake slithered behind, its shape hardly discernible in the darkness but for its head, large and well-rounded, not flat-tish at the top as the snakes he had seen, and moving quickly from side to side as its body twisted and slithered forward. The donkey cantered slowly, unhurriedly, not try-ing to escape, its pace measured as if it were accom-modating the pace of the snake which was following. It all seemed part of a game — a game of snakes and donkeys. Unsure of what to do next Granpa decided to remain behind the hedge until morning. Not that he was afraid. He just thought it best. And he was young then, less sure of himself. He curled up on the ground behind the hedge and tried to sleep but couldn't relax. He waited, listening, but there was no further sound, no clop of hoof, no patter of feet again, no neighing or braying disturbed the air. He waited until approaching daylight encouraged him to leave his hiding place, plus the fact that if he had been discovered crouching behind someone's fence at such an unaccountable time, this would indeed, have been very awkward to explain.

Granpa told no one about this. Only a few, a very few, would have believed him.

Two days later he went into Herman Deschine's shop to get some groceries. Horatio Souza came in after him and stood quietly aside until the customer then being served was walking out. Then he spoke:

"A ... aa ... " he said to Granpa: "Why you run away when you see me an' Herman the other night ... why you run away? You don't know we can't do you nothing? We only having some fun ... " He laughed throatily and continued: "Is the only time we are friends, him an me ..." He pointed his chin in Herman's direction. "Not any other time. But you run away ... " And again he laughed the throaty laughter of an old man. He looked steadily at Herman who stood transfixed on the other side of the counter, then limped out of the shop. The hatred reflected in Herman's face momentarily aged him beyond his sixty years as his eyes directed venom at Horatio's retreating figure. And Granpa's suspicions were confirmed. The rumours about Horatio and Herman took concrete shape in his mind and while Horatio busied himself with providing the goods Granpa was ordering, Granpa reflected on the tales which had spread about the two H's, as they were called — about their lifelong friendship which had turned into enmity because of treachery on the part of one of them — about their pact with the devil and the form their repayment took: becoming La Gahoos while still alive. And Granpa understood, too, what was meant by 'the other night' as he had been outside at night only once during the previous week — the night he encountered the strange combinations of animals.

As he was leaving Herman said to him, "Is better if you don't say anything about the other night. If you talk about it, perhaps you should forget to mention the stupid remark that Horatio ... stupid man ... just say ... " and his little eyes glittered with hatred, and with malice — the first directed to Horatio no doubt, the other to Granpa. As he walked out of the shop Herman's words followed him, "Good for you you can't be hurt. Good for you, you have special protection. You have the protection of one who could see but can't be touched."

Granpa never used Herman's shop again, going out of his way to purchase his requirements elsewhere, so as to keep out of the reach of one known to be a La Gahoo.

Pressed to do so, Granpa recounted to us the story of the two H's. They had been dead more than forty years, but an edifice to their entrapment still stood outside the boundary of the little village, the unfinished mansion which started deteriorating before completion and known as Herman's Folly. It was reputed to be haunted. Horatio Souza's family had come to the island from South America when he was about a year-old. They lived next door to the Deschine family and the two boys — Horatio a couple of years Herman's senior — grew up close friends. They both came from large, poor families, and naturally were forced to start contributing to the family funds while still in their youth. Things being what they were the boys of course had quite a struggle to make ends meet. Nevertheless, they were happy, and as the years rolled on they became more attached. The only slight flaw in the friendship — if one could call it that — was the fact that Maria Foderinson chose Herman instead of Horatio for her husband, although she had first started dating Horatio. The two boys were irascible and strong-willed, though Herman was the steadier and more sensible of the two. Horatio, though not quite a bully, was known to be more temperamental and inclined to have his own way whenever possible, affecting little consideration for others when his purpose was to be served. Herman, who worked in a store in town, settled down before Horatio and started a family. His ambition was to own a small dry-goods shop one day, but his goal seemed further and further away as his family grew larger and his savings smaller. By the time Horatio got married Herman and Maria had already had five children with another on the way. Horatio was a carpenter by trade. Things were not very good on the island but he made ends meet a little better than Herman, especially as he was not as progenitive. Maria Deschine was a staunch Catholic who believed that children were the gift of God and that it was her duty to carry out God's will. Not so Horatio and Sylvia. They had little use for God and his ways, more for accumulating worldly goods and enjoying the pleasures of life unhindered by his wife and rumour attributed another two or three to him, here and there on the island, as a result of favours bestowed. No one was ever sure whether these rumours could be confirmed.

And life went on day by day monotonously urgent for Herman and his brood, less so far for Horatio and his few.

The two men and their families continued to be very close, with Horatio always a little more affluent. Until a time came when he was more than just-a-little-more. He was becoming prosperous; had started a shop of his own where he employed two young cabinet makers and business grew steadily better. Herman, on the other hand, with his increasing family seemed to grow poorer until (and this was discovered long after) Horatio invited him to share in the secret of his increasing wealth.

It seemed that Horatio had discovered a book which was once owned by his great-grandfather and which had become lost amongst discarded possessions. This book gave recipes for witchcraft, how to make contact with Satan and how to 'deal' with him in order to gain power, wealth, and whatever else was desired. The only stipulation made by Satan in return for these favours was that he would ask a price, which was not known to the 'Dealer' until after the favours had been bestowed. It would appear that Horatio had called upon Satan to assist him and the result of this was that he had been improving financially. He wanted to become a councillor which would give him input into the administration of the island and was biding his time until he had become a more affluent ratepayer. Comparison was always made of the difference in positions held by the two men now, although they had started out life at par. But, people said, Maria Deschine was blest with the poor man's wealth — children. She was a blessed woman, a conscientious church-goer, etc., etc., her riches were accumulating in her home and she and her husband would reap their reward later on in their old age, etc. etc. Whilst Herman was becoming tired and a little depressed.

When Horatio, after testing him a bit, invited Herman to learn the secret of his own success, he was ripe for it. At first reluctantly, because although he was not himself religious, he still adhered to and tried to live by the principles of the church, especially as his wife was a visual reminder of these principles. But his situation being a depressing one he soon succumbed to Horatio's suggestions and in time he, too, began to be prosperous. The two men bought sweepstake tickets together, and one day they won some money. Herman had his desire, a dry-goods shop of his own. His wife helped in it occasionally between her myriad chores of child raising and the older children came in on Saturdays to assist. Soon Herman was able to build a small house and get a woman to help his wife at home.

The shop continued to prosper and expanded; his children got bicycles; his wife was better dressed. Horatio on the other hand not only owned his own home now but was buying other property and renting them. Business was booming. His children were being treated with the respect meted out to the well-to-do.

Rumours soon circulated that the men were 'dealing' — the familiar term for persons suspected of trafficking with the devil. It could be heard slyly being said: "Da man is a dealer," referring to Herman. Or, "He does deal, yer know," of Horatio. A servant employed in Horatio's house had herself seen the devil there and witnessed a ceremony held in a room which was always kept locked, when Herman and Horatio were themselves speaking to Satan. This servant who had only been employed there for a few weeks (they never kept one as the servants always seemed to be frightened away by some peculiar incident and there was a constant change of maids, gardeners and cooks) ... anyway, this particular servant who was fully aware of popular suspicions, was herself curious by nature. The room she was not allowed to enter and which was kept locked and used only by Horatio at nights, piqued her curiosity, especially when she heard strange sounds coming from there in the middle of the night. One night she tiptoed up to the room. It was about midnight, when everyone else in the house was asleep, and although the door was locked a faint light could be seen underneath. She tiptoed to the door and looked through the keyhole. At the far side of the room the blinds were drawn (it was the only room in the house with dark blinds across the windows and these were always drawn so no light entered). On the floor in the centre of the room was a low object which held a long and, to her, an oddly-shaped bulb from which came a peculiar greenish light. This flooded the room with an eerie glow. In one corner of the small, unfurnished room, stood a huge man dressed in black with a large heavy-looking cape. His oversized head seemed more like the head and face of a beast than that of a human being, and on either side of his head there were large lumps which stood out like swollen horns not yet full-grown.

She was mesmerized by the appearance of this stranger

and fascinated by the gruesomeness of his features, the large sunken eyes which emitted a purplish glow, his awesome size — he was larger than any man she had ever seen — and the dirty parchment-like quality of his skin — not really like skin at all, more like the dehydrated semblance of a mummy. Fear kept her rooted to the spot because she knew who the stranger was. She had heard the rumours. But she was also spellbound by what was taking place. Horatio, who stood naked in the centre of the room facing the stranger with outstretched arms, just stood there with a welcoming grin, almost a smile, making his face unrecognizably ugly. And Herman was there too, standing a little apart from Horatio, on the same side of the room. And he was also naked, but his arms were not outstretched in front of him like Horatio's. They were spread outward instead. He was not smiling like Horatio. He had a glazed look, as if he were entranced and waiting to be snapped out of it. The servant felt her heart pounding. She wanted to run away, to escape before they knew she was there, but she was too afraid to move. She saw the stranger turn his head in her direction, saw that he was about to speak, saw that the others were waiting for him to speak when they, too, turned towards the door and she knew, instinctively, that they had sensed her presence. She tried to straighten up from the keyhole, but her body would not move. It was as though she were rooted to the spot. She wanted to say a prayer, to call on the Holy Virgin to help her, but her tongue would not move either, it felt heavy in her mouth. She projected her thoughts outward in prayer. "Holy Virgin," she thought, "help me to escape." She prayed mentally and suddenly was able to move, just as Herman turned his body slowly in the direction of the door and was moving mechanically, but purposefully, towards it. It was if the occupants of the room had communicated mentally with each other. She heard no words, but she knew he was coming to the door because *she* was there, that he had been instructed through some form of telepathy to investigate. He was moving like a mechanized toy with arms outstretched in her direction, and the other two heads, which she could still see, were now fully turned towards her also. She tried to run away before Herman could reach the door, but there in her path was the stranger she had just turned away from in the room.

"Jesus ... Jesus ... Holy Virgin Mary ..." she screamed and ran past him, down the stairs and through the living-room. Unbolting the front door with nervous, shaking fingers, she ran screaming through the grounds and out into the street, calling out in prayer to be saved and expecting momentarily to see the huge stranger in front of her again. Uncaring as to where she was headed at the time of night. Everywhere was closed. The lights in all the houses were out. She wanted to get as far away from Horatio's house as possible.

Suddenly twin headlights swerved around the corner up ahead and she practically threw herself in front of them. It was a plantation manager on his way home. The man stopped the car and tried to speak to her. She babbled that she wanted help and could he take her away from there. The man thought she was running away from an irate husband who had been beating her. One hand was held up against her right eye, which had begun to hurt — the eye which had been looking through the keyhole.

"Where do you want to go?" the plantation manager asked, looking around briefly to make sure the suspected husband was not on her heels.

"Anywhere ..." she said, "anywhere away from here. Quick ... please ... Satan on my heels." The man wondered if she was mentally ill, or was referring to her husband as Satan. "Well ..." he said, "am going only about half a mile from here, if it's on your way I can drop you off ..." But she was already in the back of the car, sobbing hysterically. He drove away.

"Mister" she said, "please let me sleep in your kitchen

tonight ... tomorrow I'll go away ... ah'll go as far away as possible ... oney leh me sleep in your kitchen tonight ..." He felt sorry for her. Maybe his wife could handle the situation. He didn't know how to deal with this. She was now repeating that her eye was hurting.

"Do you want to go to the hospital?" he asked, still under the impression it was the work of an angry husband.

"No ... no ..." she replied. "Oney let me sleep in your kitchen tonight and tomorrow ah'll go ... please ... please ..." She pleaded pathetically and he didn't have the heart to refuse.

The story of the servant's experience spread like wildfire the next day. She slept in the plantation manager's kitchen after his wife had been told the story. Needless to say the wife didn't believe it — only thought that the woman was deranged. Nevertheless, she was allowed to remain there that night. Next day her eye was very sore. The story was repeated over and over again to those she knew personally working on the plantation and they believed her. She was afraid to return to Horatio's house for her belongings and her wages. Her brother and cousin went to the house a couple of days later, told Horatio's wife that she was in hospital and would not be returning to them. It was rumoured that she had nearly lost the sight of her right eye because the doctors did not know exactly what was wrong and weren't helping in the right way. A local healer helped her when he heard the story and although the eye was cured she was left with a slight squint. People said of it later "that was the eye she peeped at the devil with."

The servant's experience created sufficient news to last the vicinity for a few months. By constant repetition the huge stranger developed large horns about a foot or more in length. Horatio was credited with an extra eye where his navel should have been, and Herman with one large breast, plus other additions and deletions.

Herman's shop was less frequented — for a while — but as there was not much else in the way of an alternative, his customers soon crept back. Respect turned into a fearsome awe by the few. Many ignored what they heard. The servant moved to another area for fear of reprisals. Horatio and Herman continued to prosper but Horatio had to find servants outside the village. No one there would enter his house after that.

It was said that after this incident the 'dealings' often took place in Herman's house instead. Soon he began to erect a huge house about half-a-mile away from the site of the one he then occupied. His family was now considered well-to-do. He had started other businesses in other parts of the country. His nine children were the envy of many mothers. His youngest daughter, Lisa, who was at this time five-years old, was known to be his favourite. He now had seven boys and two girls. The older girl was fourteen. Lisa was always around with her father, accompanying him to the shop on the few occasions he was there (he now had someone running it for him), or waiting for him while he collected rents. Everyone knew she was his favourite.

And Herman had changed. He forbade his wife and children to attend church, saying he didn't believe in it any longer, that religion was a waste of time, that the priests and nuns were hypocrites and liars, that all anyone had to look forward to was this life and after that — nothing. His family were to enjoy all he provided for them and forget the hypocrites concerned with churches. His wife and the older children still sneaked out to church when he was away on business but they now lived an unhappy and hypocritical life. Having much more than they needed materially, they were denied the spiritual sustenance to which his wife had been accustomed. Some of the children liked him, others didn't. All sided with their mother.

Herman's attention now turned to the mansion he was building. This would put him in an even greater privileged position: the only man with such a house, not only in the neighbourhood, but possibly in the whole island, barring of course the Governor and maybe one or two others. Larger and more modern than Horatio's. His family would have all the comforts and luxuries money could provide. His wife, in the meantime, begged him not to be so foolhardy, told him that she and the children were perfectly happy with their present home and that they had more than enough for their needs. She was a charitable woman, helping the poor and anyone she knew to be in need. The more prosperous Herman became, the unhappier was his household. Though he loved his family he was blinded by greed and could not see how unhappy he was making them, especially as he forebade them associating with their church.

Horatio now sat on the City Council. Everyone voted for him because of the promises he made to improve conditions for the poor — and most of them were poor — and to help them repair their homes and build better schools. Magically, he was going to satisfy all their needs, which he promptly forgot on assuming his chair in the Council.

There were people who swore they heard odd sounds at nights coming from the homes of both Herman and Horatio. There were those who swore they 'saw' spirits wandering in and out of Herman's and Horatio's houses and businesses. There were all sorts of rumours, but the two men were now above the normal social strata of the village and continued to enjoy their wealth — until the Devil asked his price. Apparently when Herman was old and was dying he confessed everything, giving details of his and Horatio's involvement. It would appear that a human sacrifice was demanded by the devil; this was the price he asked of them both: that each would provide him with a soul. Herman was horrified. He wanted to get out of his contract. Horatio warned him that if he cancelled his contract with the devil now he stood to lose all that he had gained.

This did not sit well with Herman. He was against violence or causing physical harm to anyone. Horatio was willing to pay the price. Herman became confused and easily irritated; he didn't know what to do. He could not, he said, keep that part of the bargain, come what may. Horatio didn't want the partnership dissolved. They were in it together and he wanted it to remain that way. After much deliberation, Horatio said he found a way which would absolve them both. He would not tell Herman what it was, only that he should leave it up to him.

And this was how their friendship came abruptly to an end.

One day Herman's little girl, Lisa, was missing. A thorough search was made for her. The child had never wandered off before. She never went far from the house alone. Every hollow, every patch of bush was searched, and every house where the owner may have been away for the day. Bus drivers were questioned and people on the streets. Every possible means was used to try and find her. But without success. That night was to be one of the pre-arranged rendezvous nights for Herman and Horatio with their hellish conspirator. Herman said he would ask their benefactor if he could tell him where his daughter was. He was distraught because he loved the child very much. Horatio suggested he should skip that night and continue instead with the search for Lisa and he, Horatio, would put the question for him. He reminded Herman that they were like brothers and it would be just as well if he asked in Herman's place. Already worried about the pact he did not want to keep, plus the additional concern about the missing child which filled his mind, Herman was glad to agree.

Night fell and still no success in locating Lisa. In his distraught, restless state, Herman had second thoughts about the request Horatio would make on his behalf and decided to go over to Horatio's house early in the evening in order to tell him that he did not just want the devil to tell him where the child was, but actually help him to locate her. In return he would seriously consider what was asked of him — the sacrifice of another human. Lisa was the light of his life and he felt that if necessary he would commit himself on her account.

Usually they met in the secret room at midnight, when there was less threat of disturbance by any of the household. Never had they met before that hour. When Herman arrived at Horatio's house his wife told him that Horatio was secreted in the private room. No one had ever been permitted to enter apart from the two H's, and although Horatio's wife suspected what took place when he said he used the room to 'meditate' she herself had never been permitted entry.

Herman went to find him. He, also, used the room so there was no compunction on his part about entering while Horatio was there, never suspecting that at that particular moment their unearthly visitor was also there. Horatio had in fact, called on him earlier than usual. He was not taking any chances in case Herman had changed his mind about being at the rendezvous. Fortunately the door was unlocked. Perhaps this was an oversight on Horatio's part owing to the haste with which he wanted to get the matter over with, or perhaps it was a quirk of Fate. Anyway, as Herman softly opened the door the sight which met his eyes left him completely dumbfounded but he was soon galvanized into action. Just in time. One more second and it would have been too late. Horatio stood in the centre of the room. The devil was in his usual position in the corner with a ludicrous grin depicting his approval of Horatio's action. And in Horatio's upraised arms was Lisa, naked, with mouth bandaged and her legs tied together at the ankles. Her arms were flailing the air helplessly, as she was suspended over a contraption of some sort on which lay the sharp, glittering blade of a cutlass, upturned and waiting to impale the helpless child. Halted abruptly by the shock of what he was witnessing Herman moaned his friend's name in one long, drawn-out sound. A magnified whisper ''Horatio ...'' was all he could moan.

Then he threw himself at Horatio with such force that the two men fell heavily to the floor, while the child dropped from Horatio's arms with all the force with which he meant her to be impaled. But she fell to the floor instead of the cutlass. The sudden appearance of Herman, his speedy action, the forceful impact with which he collided with Horatio, all contributed to impeding his aim. The two men grappled, Herman trying to strangle Horatio and Horatio fighting for his life at the hands of the enraged Herman. Meanwhile the devil stood his ground and laughed heartily, gruesomely "Ha..ha..ha..aaaa..ha..ha..ha..aaa..aaa.. ha..haa..ha..ha..haaaaaa..ha..ha..aaa..ha..ha..haaaa.. ha..ha.." as though he were being tickled by giant fingers and obviously enjoying the spectacle. Herman remembered the child, and letting go of Horatio he ran and lifted her off the ground where she lay quite still. Without hesitation he left the room cradling Lisa and looking anxiously down at her pale face. He didn't know whether she was still alive, whether the fall had injured her or whether in fact, any other injury had been done to her before his arrival. He ran out of the house, jumped into his waiting car and sped to his doctor's home. Not until fifteen minutes later, when he arrived at the doctor's house, did he remove the bandages. Her eyes were still closed but she was moaning softly and tossing on the back seat where she lay.

Herman did not tell the doctor the truth — only that he found her lying in a deep ditch. On examination it was found that her spine was injured. For six months Lisa lay in the children's ward of the general hospital. And gossip was rife with speculation as to the truth of the matter. Someone had seen Herman run out of the house with the naked child in his arms ... someone contradicted the statement that she had been found in a ditch ... someone speculated as to the truth of the matter.

When it was discovered that Horatio and Herman's friendship had been severed, someone put two and two together and came up with sixty-one rumours, speculations, ideas and surmises. It was even suggested that Horatio, who owned race horses, had kidnapped the little girl and kept her hidden in his house prior to cutting out her heart to feed his racehorses. To the accompaniment of some form of 'simidimi' of course. This was known to stimulate a horse to such an extent that it would run faster than its normal speed and therefore easily win a race. But it had to be the heart of a young child. Others suggested that Horatio had bad habits which Granpa would not explain to us. There were suggestions, too, that Horatio was very fond of the child. She called him 'Godfather' though by the time she was born Herman had forbidden his wife to have the younger children christened. Others said that he wanted her to live with him but her parents would not give her away. Rumours ... rumours ... a confusion of rumours circulated.

Meanwhile, the big house Herman was building was nearly completed (Horatio had already been living in a palatial affair).

The two men did not speak to each other again. At least not openly, though they met secretly for their devilry, at the home of one or the other, despite the fact that each by this time was conducting his individual rendezvous with the evil one. They had not yet paid the price. Horatio had been thwarted in his effort which he tried to explain to Herman would have benefited them both — Horatio by committing the act, and Herman, through the sacrifice of what he loved most. Horatio explained that he had set this up with Satan after suggesting something along those lines to Herman, who had been stunned at his friend's even thinking, far less mouthing, such a plan. Horatio had said to Herman that as he had so many children, one less would not have mattered and his wife need never know. He, Horatio, had only two, therefore one would be missed. At Herman's reaction to this, Horatio acted as if he had been making fun and treated it all as a joke.

Herman tried to back out of his arrangements with

Horatio and the devil, offering to give up all he owned, but was told it was too late. He had enjoyed the fruits of his endeavours. The price must be paid regardless of whether he kept those fruits or not. He had them on trust. They could not be returned to the supplier. A price must be paid whether he backed out or stayed in. (All this was confessed by Herman at the end.)

Herman's businesses suddenly began to fail. The cause was said to be that he was now neglecting them and spending too much time at the hospital with his daughter. Rats were seen running about the shop and customers went in only when it was unavoidable. Part of the structure of the new house collapsed, injuring a workman. Work slowed down as investigations were made. A stranger opened another shop nearby and business was transferred almost suddenly from Herman's to the new one, which was more modern as well. Still, he had other investments and could survive. Horatio, too, began to suffer financial losses. His horses died mysteriously, said to have been poisoned by rival racehorse owners. His son contracted polio and at nine became a cripple despite the best medical services his father's money could buy. And so it went on. In the meantime, Herman was having additional problems. The day his daughter left the hospital using crutches, his wife left home taking all the children.

Maria had suspected for a long time what the two H's' were up to, but her suspicions were only confirmed when her distraught husband blurted out the situation in which he had found Lisa and threatened to kill Horatio for it. She asked him to let her return to the church openly and to try and help him break the arrangement he had. He was only too glad to do this but could not really cut himself off completely from his dealings. So the ensuing conflict greatly widened the already widening rift between them.

Herman could not find out where his family had gone. They were not with his wife's parents who were living in the South. It was said that she had gone to Venezuela to her brother and his family. Herman went there, but did not find them. He had no way of knowing either how Lisa was, whether she was walking any better, or whether her back remained badly damaged. Bereft of family and without his lifelong friend, Herman soon began to give up — especially as business was lagging. No way could he finish the house, much as he wanted to, much as it would have been a monument to his success. No matter what efforts were expended, what materials used, what new contractors was brought in, something always went wrong and month after month went by with no sign of the house being completed.

Horatio's business picked up, but not completely — and Herman knew that Horatio had tried to pay the price when the body of a young boy was discovered not far from his home, with the throat slit. Herman suggested to the police that they question Horatio, but without any tangible evidence he was accused of being envious of his friend because his own businesses were failing. Horatio only smiled when Herman accused him of the murder. But it was too late. The devil had only been biding his time and having a little game with them. Herman had not yet paid the price. Horatio had failed miserably in his first attempt and this carried a penalty, so they were both condemned to roam in the form of animals, and no matter how much they hated each other they would roam together at specific times and would be powerless to do anything about it. They were free to choose whatever forms they wanted. But that was all.

As the years went by their businesses deteriorated. The house Herman was building was never completed, crumbling gradually until only a shell remained ... unused, costly, unwanted. Various attempts were made to sell the property. No one would buy it. Each time someone was interested something happened to prevent the completion of the sale. So it remained standing there unfinished. First a thing of promising beauty and grandeur, which gradually became a weather-beaten eyesore. Herman became ill, and was forced to give up his home for smaller, more economical quarters — the back of the shop, where he finally ended his days.

Horatio continued in much better circumstances for a while — only for a while for he, too, soon felt the effects of the curse which had been placed upon him. His wife died and his daughter ran away. Horatio was left with a crippled son to look after who could in no way ever earn a living for himself. Horatio became more irascible as he grew older but with a bitter humour and eventually was jailed for two years for some fraudulent involvement. His businesses deteriorated faster while he was away. But that was the only peace he was destined to know, because while there it was not possible to leave at will in order to roam the streets at night with his companion — although on one occasion his cellmate reported he had been missing for four hours but mysteriously reappeared. He never knew the explanation.

During that time Herman wandered alone except on the one occasion Horatio was able to join him. A huge dark shape like an oversized monkey was sometimes seen. But no one ever came close enough to it to know exactly what it was. Often it would be heard making sad, lonely noises and skipping about restlessly. On Horatio's release they again took up their nightly escapades, which went on for some considerable time, including the time when Granpa had seen them on Hallowe'en. They did not go out every night, only on certain occasions, like when the moon was full, or Hallowe'en, or other times known to be propitious for hauntings and the haunted.

Herman died first, many years later. Quite some time after the incident Granpa had witnessed. The men were still bitter enemies, avoiding each other as much as possible, meeting only when their sin of dealing with the devil had to be expiated, when they would roam as animals.

Granpa was reluctant to tell us more — about how

Herman died and what happened at the time, how his family came back briefly into his life or, more appropriately, his death, and how Horatio's turn came. But we pestered him relentlessly until he did. I suspect now that he wanted the pleasure of being asked to continue, because, in fact, I'm sure he would at some other time have taken up the story again, the rest was too good to be ignored completely.

One day a nun arrived in the village, or rather two nuns, although the older one remained in the car which brought them, together with the driver. It was a hired car. The younger nun got out and walked a few yards to Herman's shop. She stood looking at it doubtfully as if she was unsure of whether it was the place she wanted. The doors were open, and flies buzzed around one doorway where a bag of sugar rested. After some hesitation she entered. It was Lisa. When she had left there as a child the shop was modern and well-kept. Now, after fourteen years, the place was unrecognizable. Its general dilapidation and the dirt clinging to the unwashed floors and the outside of the building had transformed it completely. There was only one person inside waiting to be served — an old woman who had known Lisa as a child but who did not recognize her at first. A nun entering Herman's dirty shop was a sight in itself, but asking if this was Herman Deschine's place, and standing aside waiting patiently for Herman to come in from the backroom where he had gone for a piece of salted meat, was something else. The nun stood patiently waiting for the customer to leave and Herman scowled at the sight of her, while he wrapped the salted meat in newspaper and handed it to the woman. The woman made a fetish of getting out some money from a little cloth sack pulled from her bosom, spending more time than necessary counting and separating the coins, and even after Herman had placed them in the grubby till she hesitated, waiting no doubt for Herman and the nun to speak.

"Father ...?" the nun said hesitantly, "It's me, Lisa ..."

"Lisa ...?" Herman repeated ... "Lisa?"

The nun shook her head and moved closer to the counter. They both ignored the woman who stood near the doorway making no attempt to leave. As a matter of fact she immediately turned back and exclaimed,

"Lisa ... little Lisa?" She held out one free hand and Lisa took it, asking if she was Ma Ellen who lived in the alley long ago when she was a child.

Ma Ellen shook her head and there were tears shining in her eyes, "Little Lisa ... a nun ..." and she shook her head unbelievingly again. Lisa was not so little now, ensconced in folds of black serge. But the noticeable limp with which she walked gave her a slightly shorter appearance. When Ma Ellen's discretion prevailed on her to leave them alone she reluctantly left to spread the news and bring all available to the spot to see "Little Lisa ... a nun."

Herman had been standing looking at Lisa the nun with a tinge of incredulity — not because she was a nun, he had known this — but that she had come there to see him. He had eventually found his family years later. They had been sent to school in Barbados after going first to their grandparents in the South. Their uncle in Venezuela had been prepared to keep them in school there away from their own island, when he learnt of the circumstances under which they had been taken away from home. His wife, after going to New York for a short while, had returned to the island unknown to Herman and stayed with her parents while the children grew up and dispersed: some overseas, some to return to the island.

From an early age Lisa had decided she wanted to become a nun and on completing her education she returned to stay with her mother for a short while, then entered a convent when she was 18. All this Herman had learnt after they had grown up and started their own lives, ignoring him completely. His wife would not see him. He tried to see Lisa once at the convent but she was in Retreat and could not see visitors. He never went back and now nearly two years later here she was, visiting him.

Lisa had been on his conscience more than anyone else. Whilst in hospital the doctors had said that walking would be hampered by the injury to her spine. He knew she was walking with crutches when she left the hospital but never learnt much more.

It would appear that Lisa felt it was her duty to forgive her father — if indeed he was responsible for what had happened to her as a child (her mother had told her) and, too, to find out the truth of the matter for some of it seemed incredible to her. There was in her mind only a vague memory of being taken to Uncle Horatio's home to which she was accustomed to going anyway, and of the horror of being tied and lifted in the air after she had been locked up for some time in a cupboard, without seeing anyone else, least of all Horatio's children, with whom she was used to playing.

Now with tears in his eyes, Herman asked her to leave, saying it was no place for her to be visiting — and no doubt embarrassed at the changed circumstances in which she found him. At first he denied the story her mother had told her, then shamefacedly, confessed the truth of it. He said he had reformed and had discontinued his dealings with the devil (he did not tell her of his being a La Gahoo). She promised to pray for him and invited him to visit her, assuring him that she would come to see him whenever she could.

Lisa's visit disturbed Herman very much. Apart from the fact that she was his favourite and he was very touched by her coming, he had been warned to stay away from anyone or anything concerned with religion and the churches. Although it was his daughter, he did not know how either Horatio or the devil would react to this because they, and especially Satan, knew every move he made. But he was glad to see Lisa ... Lisa his favourite. He had not seen any of the others since they left.

Herman and Horatio's deaths also provided a distraction for the villagers. When it was realized that Herman was dying, after a short illness, a neighbour sent for the priest. Most people had been keeping away from the two H's and by this time they were living lonely lives. But there were those who felt it their Christian duty to look after the souls of the lost, and one such person was Herman's next door neighbour, a kindly soul who, despite all that she had heard about the two H's, and in spite of the vicarious sounds and carryings-ons which emanated from his house from time to time, summoned the priest when she felt he was about to draw his last breath. The priest was not available. He had been out on extended visits. Herman, who by this time had been mentally softened up did not oppose the suggestion. He, too, knew it was the end. Unfortunately, the priest could not get there in time. Desperate for absolution, Herman confessed to the neighbour all that he had been involved in, and expressed the wish that his body should be given the last rites of the church, despite the fact that he had become a heretic. He knew this would please his daughter Lisa, and felt that he was doing it more for her's than his own sake. A wake was kept that night as was customary. Although few people came to keep vigil, there were those who thought it unfit that a body — anybody's body — should be left on its own during its last night on earth, so they came to watch, and to make coffee, and eat biscuits and cheese, and to pray, and to gossip.

Among these were the curious. But there were also those who refused to go near the house, suggesting that anyone who did was keeping vigil with the devil. And there were those, too, who thought it their duty to attend every wake in the village. It was, for them, a pastime. Whereas each and every mobile adult would have called to pay his respects, had it been someone else, very few indeed came. And so it was that only a handful of people were present when Horatio turned up. And he was drunk.

Whatever else he had been known to be in life that was unsavoury, he had never been known to be a drunkard, or to touch liquor at all for that matter. Now here he was, staggeringly drunk. Also, everyone knew that he and Herman had been enemies over the years. His presence now, in the face of death, was a greater mystery. The simpler, and more kindly of those present, attributed his visit to nostalgia for their one-time youthful friendship. They said he came to pay his last respects, forgetting the immediate past and remembering only their boyhood, and that was the reason for his being drunk — because Herman had died before they had become reconciled.

Imagine their surprise when Horatio stationed himself at the foot of the large, ice-packed casket and with arms outstretched towards the body began to grimace and growl like an animal. Imagine their surprise when the casket started vibrating. All present remarked, next day, how they felt a sudden iciness descend upon the room. One old man who had been dozing was startled into alertness and shouted 'earthquake' on seeing the casket rocking. Fear descended on all. One or two swore they saw the head and shoulders of the dead rising slowly, but that they did not wait to see anymore. They fled. Except the kindly neighbour who was known to be near-sighted and a little deaf, and a young man who was too terrified to move and who remained frozen in his chair. The casket continued to rock and he saw (so he said) the eyes of the dead man slowly opening. Next day two pennies were placed on the eyes and they were bandaged to keep them closed. Some people claimed they had never been properly shut. The young man and the neighbour apparently realised, more or less at the same time, that they were the only ones left and, holding hands, they too fled, abandoning the deceased to whatever wiles were to be exercised by Horatio.

Needless to say, on the following day there was a large audience witnessing the small funeral procession to the church and nearby cemetery. As a rule most people would have attended the funeral, especially as the deceased had been born and had lived all his life in the village. But they participated instead as onlookers. The tale of the previous night's incidents had already been circulated, rehashed and embroidered. The long pathway leading to the church was lined with people. Only a small cortege followed the hearse and amongst them were three of Herman's sons, and Lisa, accompanied by another nun. It was this which had really brought people out in full force, to see Herman's grown children who, except for Lisa, had never returned, and to see in particular Lisa, the nun. There was no doubt in anyone's mind but that Lisa had encouraged her brothers to attend. Her mother was already dead and the other children were overseas.

As the small procession was halfway up the paved aisle to the church there was some commotion. The horses came to a halt and would not go forward. They pawed the ground, attempted to turn back, even tried to go in different directions although they were harnessed together. Various interpretations were given to this, that the body did not want to enter a church, that the horses could see the spirit of Herman leading the cortege (it was known that this often happened, as was described by those versed in clairvoyance) and various other opinions. In order to save time the coffin was removed from the hearse but the bearers, including Herman's sons, didn't make much headway. First, one handle of the coffin became loose, making it awkward to be carried. Then, for no apparent reason, the coffin seemed to twist itself to one side as though the weight became heavier there, although there was no room for the body to shift inside. In order to adjust this they lay it on the ground, but on lifting it again (and no one knew exactly what happened) it overturned and Herman fell out face down.

Lisa was the only one who wept while she fingered the beads hanging at her side.

Horatio was in the audience. He stood near the street,

furthest away from the church. No one stood near him. As soon as he was recognised those who were nearby moved away, but darted furtive glances in his direction, remembering what they had been told of the previous night's incidents, wondering what he was thinking, studying him, and surmising ... always surmising. Wondering, too, what took place in the empty room where Herman's body was left alone with him the night before. Horatio looked drawn and tired. His face was a pale ugly mask and the lines around his mouth were taut. He looked at no one. His eyes squinted in the direction of the moving cortege as though he were straining to see every movement ahead. As though he were thoughtfully working out a puzzle.

As the bearers neared the opened doorway of the church there suddenly appeared on the upper step a huge man in dark clothes, an old-fashioned cape adding incongruity to his dress. Some did not see his face clearly, others said they were aware of large eyes — larger than any human eyes they had ever seen — bulging gruesomely out of his face. The bearers halted, thinking someone had come out of the church to meet them. The huge stranger lifted his arms and spread them out, like wings, lifting the folds of his cape, until he resembled a monstrous bird which was attempting to block the doorway of the church. No one knew what to do. It was such a strikingly unpleasant sight. And a strange one. Lisa moved forward and stood in front of the coffin, lifting her beads and plying them swiftly between her fingers, while her lips moved soundlessly. Some felt, then, that there was hope after all for Herman's soul because his daughter was a nun and she would pray ceaselessly for him. Behind the large stranger, the priest, who doubtless had been waiting for some time, for the procession was late, emerged with an acolyte, and immediately they came out of the church door the stranger disappeared. There were many who wondered if the priest had seen the stranger at all as he walked forward and waited on the steps to receive the body and escort it inside. Everyone said that Lisa knew who the stranger was — she had seen him as a child.

As soon as the stranger appeared on the church steps Horatio slinked away.

No one thought about him again for a while, until some days later when his body was discovered wedged behind a cupboard door in his house, as though he had been trying to hide from someone. He had obviously died during the night of Herman's funeral, but this was not discovered at the time (his crippled son had preceded him some years earlier). No wake was kept. The body was placed in the public mortuary and given a pauper's burial.

Many a night during the following years two strange animals could be seen roaming the streets, sometimes cantering together playfully, sometimes snarling and clawing at each other until, as time passed, only one animal roamed, making lonely pitiful noises ... and everyone said it was Horatio seeking Herman, who had by then found peace.

THE JABLESSE BAITER

The thrill of listening to twice-told tales was lessened only by the fact that we already knew the outcome. Nevertheless, we listened intently, like the time when Zeta had the measles and could not be around to hear some of them and they had to be related again for her benefit. We who had heard them before still strained and tensed. Because we had thrilled so much to the consequences we wanted to hear them again and again — ones such as incidents involving Charles Marinon, the Jablesse Baiter who boasted that he wasn't afraid of anything living or dead, and deliberately went La Jablesse hunting armed with crucifix and a small container of salt in his pocket — so he said. And Granpa chuckled as he told how once Charles was approached by a La Jablesse. Beautiful, enticing, luring him on until he felt he wanted a cigarette and took one from his pocket. On realising what he was about to do La Jablesse asked him not to smoke. She didn't like cigarette smoke, she said, it didn't agree with her. Nevertheless, unobliging as was his nature, he lit the cigarette. She immediately fell back, snarling and cursing, and he knew then who she really was. She remained standing in the street long after he had walked on and her words, wavering and slurred, reached his ears. She used the French patois familiar to the area, 'malais ... mal-eleve ... cochon d'homme ...' Her tone was peculiar, thin. He became afraid, lit two cigarettes, kept them going, lit two more before they were discarded — a safety measure. He had heard how they would stay away from smoke — and that cigarette smoke was particularly disliked or perhaps it was the scent.

Next day, and in the days and weeks which followed, Charles recounted the incident over and over again, colouring it sensationally. By the time it returned to his own ears he had become a daredevil, a defier of jablesses, one who baited, encouraged, then rebuffed them until, infused with the boldness of conceit, he became a Jablesse Baiter. Walking in lonely areas at dead of night, his defences salt, a crucifix, and the cigarettes he kept handy in the event they, too, were needed, he boasted that no Jablesse would dare to try and harm him. He related stories which some believed and some didn't, like being accosted one night by one who didn't know that he was armed (the crucifix was wrapped in silk cotton and the salt was in a tiny dried goatskin container). Their x-ray eyes couldn't pierce silk cotton or dried skin, vieux Tantante, the aged Martiniquan woman had told him. The Jablesse tried to lure him away by asking him to go with her to an old hut tucked away in the bushes as she was afraid to go alone. She had forgotten something there earlier she said and wanted to return for it.

He knew that only the local farmers used this hut if it rained while they were busy on their land and wanted to shelter. So suspecting what she was, he whipped out the crucifix from his pocket, dropped the silk cotton wrapping and held it up before her, at the same time throwing the salt at her from the skin pouch. She screamed a soul-piercing scream and seemed to shrink before his eyes, slowly, painfully, to remain stooped and growling like an animal in pain, untamed and cruel, snarling its frustration. Suddenly there appeared two more jablesses, one on either side of her, standing erect and snarling. He became afraid and backed away, the cross held high, the pouch with its remaining salt at hand. He walked backwards away from them, knowing that walking backwards would confuse anything which intended following because it would not know in which direction you were going, and confusing them this way he left, while they remained with their spoilt companion. He knew, too, that throwing salt on a jablesse spoilt her forever and she would never be able to lure anyone again. The salt on her would mysteriously spread, because of her own chemistry, and coat her in such a way that she could never again materialize once she had disappeared, that is, if she had not got enough salt on her to melt her completely. It was said that if one managed to melt a jablesse (which was rare indeed), next day you would find a puddle of water where she had been. Next morning he went back to the spot but found nothing. "So her companions took her away," he thought, for obviously, the salt had been insufficient to melt her.

After this incident he kept quiet for a while. The sudden appearance of more jablesses had intimidated him. He hadn't known they worked like that, helping each other, so he decided to lay low for a while.

Some months later he was returning home from a dance with a friend, Slim Hameth. They had dropped two girls off at their homes and, as usual, had to walk home themselves as they had no means of transport. They were both a little tipsy, a little happy. They walked along the same road where Charles had tried to melt the jablesse. They chatted about the evening, recalling the fun they'd had. Charles had arranged to meet one of the girls they had taken home the next day to go to a cinema. Slim was reiterating about his failure to 'make the grade' as he put it, with a little 'skin' — the girl with the long slim legs whom he had had his eyes on at the dance. And he hadn't quite made it. She preferred someone else ... hardly danced with him even. And he had this little regret tucked away back of his tipsy mind. Nevertheless, he had enjoyed the dance, and between them they recounted some of the funnier incidents which had taken place.

Suddenly ahead of them there appeared a line of women — four in all — strung out across the narrow road, all with straw hats shading their faces. Startled, the men stopped walking, stood where they were, watched them advancing slowly in a straight line, heard the soft drag of shoes then the stiff loud clomp of something more solid ... hooves.

"Jablesse ..." Slim screamed. Frightened into action he turned and fled as fast as his failing courage could support his legs. All tipsyness vanished as self-preservation lent strength where fear alone may have created weakness. Not Charles. His befuddled mind recounted something about a crucifix and salt. One hand dived into his pocket — a reflex action — nothing there. Nor was there any salt in a skin pouch. You didn't go to a dance and hold a girl close to the bulging discomfort of a small wooden crucifix or sack of salt. By the time he reached for cigarettes it was too late ...

And Slim kept running until the flambeau of an approaching donkey cart piled with green coconuts for the early morning market announced the approach of another human being. Slim stood in front of the donkey waving his arms up and down until the man perched on the cart pulled on the reins. Breathless from fear and exertion, Slim mumbled that he wanted a lift. Before the driver could start up again Slim had falteringly related what had happened. But the man didn't believe him. Not only had he never had the slightest belief in such nonsense, he said, but because of the smell of alcohol on Slim's breath. So he continued on his way despite Slim's efforts to make him turn back. Glad of companionship Slim went along, knowing that if the donkey sensed any inhuman presence it would show it. As they came within a short distance of where Slim had left Charles the donkey stood still, refusing to budge despite its master's coaxing, despite his efforts at pulling it forward by its halter. Ahead, and beyond the glow of the flickering flambeau, lay solid blackness. Nothingness. Yet the donkey refused to move except to trot stubbornly to the side of the road and wait. Impatiently the driver took the whip to its back. It brayed in pain and in fear but would not move forward.

"See ... what ah tell yer ..." Slim said, his fear rising again. "Ah tell yer it had some jablesses there ... leh we turn back ... don't go further ... they must be still there if Charles didn't get rid of them. He is a jablesse master but not me. I afraid of all those supernatural things." He

chided and coaxed, supporting the donkey in its stubborn-
ness. Exasperated, the driver turned the cart around and
the donkey willingly retraced its steps.

Slim stayed with the driver at his home a short distance
away, drinking coffee and eating warmed up roti, and
thinking about Charles, wondering what had taken place
in his absence. He was eager to hear what he was sure
would be a good tale of Charles' mastery of the jablesses,
but knew too, that he would not have to be ashamed
because he had run away. This was a most natural thing
to do under the circumstances. He was looking forward
to hearing Charles' account of what happened after he ran,
and decided there and then that he would willingly accept
whatever embellishments Charles might add.

As darkness dissolved and the sky lightened, the old man
decided to try once again. He was way behind his scheduled
time for the early Sunday morning market. This time there
was no hesitation on the donkey's part, as they jogged
along in the cool fresh dawn. Over the hills the distant sky
was tinged with the glow of sunrise and the sweet damp-
ness of the dew-moistened earth rose and mingled with the
heady greenness of tropical plants. A canary in the bush
sang matins, while a cocorico flitted swiftly cross their
path. And the donkey shied.

Seated next to the driver Slim snipped a brief doze from
time to time, thinking that a man could be happy on such
a morning, with the rhythmic clop, cloppity clop of the
donkey's steps and the smooth roll of the cart wheels lull-
ing him into a pleasant drowsiness, if it wasn't for the sub-
tle concern he had developed over the past few hours for
his friend. It loomed forward in his mind occasionally,
although he tried to discount it, knowing that if Charles
were unable to handle the situation he, too, should have
taken flight but wondering what he had, in fact, done.
Soon he would know! Nevertheless, there was that little
pinge of concern, although he did not know exactly why.
He dozed and woke and dozed, then avidly looked around

as they passed the place where he had left Charles ... hoping, almost expecting, to see at least one or two tiny blobs, if not a huge pool of water. But there was nothing. Not even one little stain to show that anything had even attempted to melt there. And neither the silence, nor anything visible provided evidence that he, Slim, and his friend, Charles, had actually seen four jablesses on this very spot, a few hours earlier. He debated whether he should again bring up the subject with the driver. But as he looked across at the old man who was lost in thought, his eyes looking straight ahead, his body swaying gently to the roll of the cart, seemingly oblivious of his companion, Slim thought better of it and remained silent. He began to wonder if, after all, it had really happened. Had he seen four jablesses, or had he been only hallucinating? He hadn't drunk much at the dance. Three or four shots of rum couldn't do that to him! He counselled himself to be patient, because Charles himself would soon satisfy his curiosity.

As the cart entered the neighbouring village he saw the two groups of people gathered outside the little church where early mass was about to begin. He stepped down from the cart sensing that something was wrong. Daniel, the tailor, told him what had happened. Charles' body had been found spread-eagled face down in the middle of the road. He had been taken to a hospital a few miles away where the doctor on duty said he had never before come across a case like it — every bone in the body was broken, every limb stretched out of its socket, and there was neither scratch, nor dent, nor tear in the skin, or a spot of blood present to indicate how it had happened.

GLOSSARY

bake: A dough made with baking powder or soda. It is sometimes baked as a large, round, flat bread or in small portions on a griddle (known as a platen), or fried.

breadfruit: A large, round, tropical vegetable; tree-grown; green-skinned with firm greyish-white flesh, which turns a pale yellow when cooked.

carat (roof): Roofing made with an overlay of dried palm leaves, once common with wattle structures, or white-washed clay; often built low over tightly packed, smooth earth which was swept clean daily.

cocoyea (broom): Dried central rib of palm fronds, stripped and tied together in bunches for use as brooms.

cocrico: Tropical bird.

Jablesse: Patois of the French 'Diablesse' — Devilwoman.

La Gahoo: Patois of the French 'Loup Garoo' — Werewolf.

mirasmee: A medical term (no longer used) for ex-
(malnutrition) tremely anaemic children. This sometimes caused excemas or a rash.

pap: Porridge of any kind.

parlour: Small foodstore where sweets, soft drinks and breads are sold.

raise his nose: Used to indicate that pride in another (usually one's children) is likely to encourage a nose-in-the-air attitude.

shop: Small grocery, or dry-goods store.

simidimi: A summing-up term for any kind of ritual which cannot be easily defined, or of which only a hazy knowledge is available.

soucouya: Patois of 'Succion' — sucking, from
(also Soucouyant) the French "to suck". (Though thought by some to be a distortion of 'suckin ya', as spoken by African tongues.) West Indian Vampire — but with no claim to immortality.

sweetbread: A cake-type bread made with yeast, dried fruit and desiccated coconut, or coconut milk.

Tey-Ley-Ley: African print. Once the cheapest cotton material available.

Verte-Ver: Dried root of a tropical, aromatic
(Vetevay) grass which, when used for scrubbing floors, keeps away insects and leaves a pleasant, almost clinical scent.

GRANPA

We had our own special Storyteller, my friends and I. He wasn't a grandfather at all in his own rights. Yet he was a grandfather to all. I didn't even know his name until after his death. He was always just "Granpa" to everyone, adults as well as children.

He spent long hours sitting with us at the front of my home on the long, lazy afternoons, scaring the life out of us when he pretended that the things he said had really happened; that the legendary figures of La Jablesse and Jumbie were real and that he had known, or still knew, some of the characters involved in the tales.

Our regular group consisted of Alan, Zeta, Donald and my sister Rita and I, who ranged in age from 11 (I was the youngest) to 13 — Donald and Rita.

Whilst most of us knew the legends, the stories within which they were interwoven for us were new.

When Granpa died we lost not only a dear friend, but a means of entertainment.

I have never forgotten him. As time passed the urge grew stronger to chronicle his narrative and to relive those wonderfully tense moments he provided.